INTRODUCTION TO SPORTS TRAINING

INTRODUCTION TO SPORTS TRAINING

T.K. Narasimham

CRESCENT
PUBLISHING CORPORATION

[*The responsibility for the facts stated, conclusions reached and plagiarism, if any, in this book is entirely that of the Author. And the Publisher bears no responsibility for them, whatsoever.*]

Introduction to Sports Training

First Published : 2009

ISBN 978-81-8342-115-7

Published by :

CRESCENT PUBLISHING CORPORATION
4831/24, Prahlad Street,
Ansari Road, Darya Ganj,
New Delhi - 110002
Ph. : 23272541, 23257835
Fax : 91-011-23257835
e-mail : campusbooks@hotmail.com

Printed at :
Roshan Offset Printers
Delhi

Preface

The aim of sport training is to help students become both skilled sports participants and 'good sports'. Rather than simply teaching the basic skills, sport training involves students in all aspects of their selected sport. They learn to play, coach, referee, and manage. With the help of sport training, students develop skill and fitness specific to particular sports, experience the social and personal values playing a sport can provide and develop the capacity to make reasoned decision about issues in sport.

This book is written for individuals interested in sports and sports training. It focuses on the basic aspects of sports training. It brings within its purview not just the rigmarole of training activities, but also the issues that surround it, such as education for trainers, diet and exercise, better organisation and funds for sports training etc.

The book tries to familiarise the readers with the working of sports training, and acquaint them with what entails imparting and receiving training in a particular sporting activity. Taking into amount current trends, development and practices, it also makes a thorough assessment of the evolving changes in sports training. It is hoped that the incisive and comprehensive content of the book serves well for the people.

T.K. Narasimham

Contents

	Preface	*v*
1.	Strength Training	1
2.	Speed Training	55
3.	Power Training	81
4.	Weight Training	113
5.	Agility Exercises	125
6.	Plyometric Training	139
7.	Flexibility Training	173
8.	Endurance Training	198
9.	Baseball Training	219
10.	Golf Fitness	231
11.	Soccer Training	254
	Bibliography	276
	Index	278

1

Strength Training

The benefits of strength training to athletic performance are enormous and many. Not only is it an integral conditioning component for power athletes such as football and rugby players, performance in the pure endurance events can be improved with a well-structured strength routine. However, aside from perhaps bodybuilders, sport-specific resistance training requires a more refined approach than simply lifting heavy weights to complete exhaustion.

A physiological analysis of any game or event will confirm that most athletes require explosive power, muscular endurance, maximal strength or some combination of all three in order to excel. Rarely is pure muscle bulk the primary concern and when it is, other elements of strength are equally as important.

Elements of a Strength Training Program

Hypertrophy

Synonymous with most people's perception of strength training, hypertrophy refers to increased muscle bulk and size. This is only one aspect of a sport-specific strength training program and one that should be included for only a select group of athletes. Football and rugby players require significant bulk to withstand very aggressive body contact. For most athletes however, too much muscle bulk is a hindrance. And remember that a larger muscle is not necessarily a stronger muscle.

Maximal strength

Maximal strength is the highest level of force an athlete can possibly generate. Its importance will vary between sports but this relates more to the length of the maximal strength training phase than whether it should be included or not. The greater an athlete's maximal strength to begin with, the more of it can be converted into sport-specific strength endurance or explosive power. Maximal strength training can improve exercise economy and endurance performance. Interestingly, it does not appear to lead to a significant increase in muscle hypertrophy.

Explosive power

Rarely is an athlete required to produce a singular maximal effort in their sport. With the exception of powerlifting, most sports require movements that are much more rapid and demand a higher power output than is generated during maximal lifts. So while maximal strength training lays an important foundation increasing the potential for additional power development, if there is no conversion of this strength into sport-specific power, the program as a whole is much less effective.

An athlete can be exceptionally strong but lack substantial power due to an inability to contract muscle quickly. Power training is used to improve the rate of force production and a range of methods such as plyometrics can be employed to convert maximal strength into explosive power.

Strength endurance

Explosive power is not always the predominant goal of the strength training program. For events such as distance running, cycling, swimming and rowing, strength endurance is a major limiting factor. Again, the greater amount of starting maximal strength, the more of it can be maintained for a prolonged period. Strength endurance can be developed through circuit training or the use of low weights and high repetitions. However, many strength endurance programs are inadequate for endurance-based sports - a set of 15-20 repetitions for example does not condition the neuromuscular system in the same way as a long distance event.

Periodisation

The concept of periodisation is key to sport-specific strength training. Dividing the overall training plan into succinct phases or periods, each with a specific outcome, allows sport-specific strength to peak at the right times, whilst minimising the risk of over-training.

It also allows more specific elements of strength to be built on a solid and more general fitness foundation. Athletes cannot progress week-in week-out indefinitely so periodisation permits variations in intensity and volume to promote performance enhancements for as long as possible.

The Sport Specific Approach to Strength Training Programs

Sport-specific strength training programs are fundamental to an athlete's development and success. Long gone are the days when coaches shunned weight lifting for fear that it might hinder the performance of fine skill and correct technique. It's now accepted that high levels of strength are a prerequisite to superior speed, power, strength endurance and overall sporting performance. Unfortunately, most strength training programs fall well short of what an athlete requires bodybuilding and Olympic weightlifting programs still dominate many athletes' training regimes. While these types of training have their place, strength training for sport consists of a more refined approach than simply lifting heavy weights as many times as possible.

This chapter outlines the concept and the benefits of a periodised strength training plan. This is the most effective approach to strength training for sport. Not only does it help in the prevention of over training, it gives the athlete the best chance of peaking physically at the right time.

Exercise selection

The principle of specificity states that training should mirror the demands of the sport as closely as possible. This applies not only to way the body's energy systems and neuromuscular system is taxed (through manipulation of intensity and rest intervals etc) but also to the movement patterns of each exercise.

Bodybuilders tend to isolate a muscle group and work it to exhaustion. Athletes on the other hand should train movements rather than muscles. A simple example is the vertical jump. The muscles involved in this action (calves, quadriceps, hamstrings, gluteals etc.) could be trained separately with exercise choices such as toe raises, leg extensions, leg curls, kickbacks and so on. A more appropriate exercise however is a barbell squat, which closely matches the movement pattern of the vertical jump. Taken a step further, jump squats are even more specific to jumping and it's not surprising that they increase vertical jump performance to the greatest extent.

Athletes must divide their time and energy amongst various types of training - endurance, strength and power, speed and agility, tactical etc., and find the time to recover! By choosing only the most appropriate resistance exercises volume can be kept to a minimum saving energy for other types of training. This has led many coaches to incorporate Olympic weight lifting into their strength training programs, almost without question. The rationale is that just a few Olympic lifts will build all-round strength and power. Whilst exercise such as power cleans can be beneficial to some athletes, for many there are more specific and more appropriate options.

Many of the sample strength training programs within this section of the website consist of relatively few exercises. This is deliberate and while it may seem unbalanced at first glance, it takes into account other training the athlete is expected to complete.

Different Types of Strength Training

Unlike bodybuilding, where the only aim is to increase the size and appearance of muscles, strength training programs for sport ultimately must develop either explosive power or muscular endurance. However, rather than immediately embarking on a program to improve either or both of these fitness components, a more effective approach is to first build a solid foundation...

Basic Strength

Basic strength training programs adapt the body for more strenuous resistance training later on. It's objective is to prepare the body by targeting all of the major muscle groups, tendons, ligaments and joints helping to prevent injury.

The less experienced an athlete is, the more time they will need to spend developing foundational strength before progressing onto more advanced forms of resistance training. But even experienced athletes should set aside some time during the year to complete a phase of basic strength training. It can help to redress some of the muscle imbalances that inherently occur with competitive sport.

Hypertrophy

Some athletes will benefit from increasing their lean body mass by adding extra muscle bulk. However, the number of athletes that require hypertrophy training or a phase of bodybuilding is far fewer than most would expect. Larger muscles are not necessarily stronger and more weight - even lean, active weight - can be a hindrance in many sports.

Maximal strength

Bodybuilders have exceptional muscle mass but they are typically bigger than they are strong. Maximal strength training programs do not necessarily increase the size of a muscle (hypertrophy) but they do lead to neuromuscular adaptations that are favourable to most athletes. Even endurance athletes can benefit from maximal strength training.

Explosive power

Just as an athlete can be extremely muscular and lack an associated level of strength, they can also be exceptionally strong but lack significant power. Most athletic movements occur much more rapidly and demand significantly more power than lifting maximal loads. If maximal strength is not converted into sport-specific power, athletic performance will not improve - certainly not to the extent that it could.

Muscular endurance

While many sports are dominated by powerful, explosive

actions some athletes are required to overcome a relatively low resistance but for a prolonged period of time. Just as power athletes should convert maximal strength into explosive power, endurance athletes should aim to convert maximal strength into muscular endurance. Of course, many team sports require a combination of the two - power and strength endurance - and developing both simultaneously without one negating the other requires careful consideration.

The Periodisation of Strength

To promote long term training improvements and avoid over training, an overall training program can be split into specific periods, each with their own objectives and set of training parameters. This concept is called periodisation and it is the most effective approach to planning strength training programs for sport. The overall training program (usually taken as one year long) can be split into set periods and usually consist of the:

— Preparation Period (Pre-season)

— Competition Period (In-season)

— Transition Period (Off / closed-season)

By co-ordinating the different elements of a strength training program with the phases of a typical season, the athlete can reach a peak for the start of the competitive season and most important parts of year. Just as an overall season is split into distinct periods or phases so is the development of sport-specific strength. As mentioned earlier, it makes sense to develop certain types of strength before others. Here are the phases, in order, of an overall strength training program (which also lasts a year) and how they should coincide with phases of a typical season above:

Phase 1 - Basic strength

Training for many sports can have an unbalancing effect on the body's musculoskeletal system. One side of the body may become stronger than the other, agonists may be overly strong compared to antagonists and smaller muscle groups are often neglected. Left unchecked these imbalances can compound and may lead to chronic and acute injury. A period of basic strength training should occur at the start of the preparation period (early pre-season). For less experienced athletes it may be necessary to start during the transition period (closed season).

Phase 2 - Maximum strength / hypertrophy

Most athletes benefit from a period of maximal strength training. The length of this phase will vary depending on the sport. Strength and power athletes will spend more time in this phase compared to endurance athletes for example. If a period of hypertrophy training is required (i.e. football or rugby players) it usually occurs before maximal strength training. Hypertrophy and maximal strength training programs usually occur midway through the preparation phase (pre-season).

Phase 3 - conversion

Until this point strength training has been generic in nature. To be effective however, this general base of strength must converted into sport-specific power or muscular endurance or both. The conversion of maximal strength occurs late in the preparation phase and may continue into the start of the competitive season.

Phase 4 - Maintenance

When strength training stops the benefits gained previously quickly diminish. In order to avoid this detraining effect a certain level of conditioning is required to maintain the gains made in the preparation phase. Fortunately, the volume required to maintain strength is less than that required to build it. But with the onset of competitive matches and events, plus a greater emphasis on tactical and skill-based training, less time is available for strength conditioning and sufficient recovery. The maintenance phase occurs throughout the competitive season.

Phase 5 - Active recovery

Following a strenuous season, a break from structured training and the rigours of competition is crucial for physical and mental respite. This can mean a complete break from all types of strength training programs for several weeks. Any longer than 3-4 weeks however, and fitness, particularly strength and power, diminishes rapidly. The active recovery phase occurs in the transition period (off / closed season).

Step-By-Step Strength Training Programs

We have recently developed an extensive range of strength training workouts and training plans for both sport and general fitness. Using proven sports-science principles each plan comes with complete sets, reps and animated exercise images. You'll find various types of programs to suit your needs such as:

— Free weights routines
— Medicine ball workouts
— Bodyweight only programs
— Sandbag workouts
— Kettlebell routines
— Sports-specific strength plans
— Plus dozens of audio interviews with the world's top strength coaches

How to Design a Resistance Training Program for Your Sport

Resistance training is now accepted as an integral and crucial part of any athlete's training plan. Unlike the generic strength training routines found in fitness magazines, sport-specific strength conditioning involves a few more design variables and takes a little more planning. This guide outlines the seven steps to designing effective resistance training programs for sport.

Step 1 - Evaluation and assessment

The first step, and perhaps the most important, is to evaluate the characteristics of the sport and to assess the athlete's physical profile.

Evaluating the sport

Ultimately, a resistance training program should mirror the movement patterns of the sport as closely as is feasible. While early stages of the program may focus on developing a general strength base, as the competitive season approaches, conditioning exercises should become more specifically tailored to the sport. The same applies to the physiological demands of the sport - a cross country runner for example, requires high levels of muscular endurance. A volleyball player would benefit from explosive power and a football lineman from exceptional muscle mass. A hockey player would benefit from basic strength, explosive power and strength endurance.

Assessing the athlete

A conditioning plan is only as successful as the individual's ability to commit to it. For most, training time is limited so the key is to prioritise. Although in an ideal scenario a soccer player would benefit from addressing explosive power and strength endurance needs, their lack of physical size and strength may be their greatest hindrance. A program to bulk the player up may have the greatest impact on their performance. The only way to ascertain the most appropriate program design is through a battery of fitness tests. Again, selection of appropriate tests comes from an evaluation of the sport.

As a rule of thumb one repetition maximum testing for the upper and lower body is appropriate for most sports. The standing vertical jump is an obvious power test for a basketball player. The 60-second sit-up or push-up test would be suitable for many of the endurance sports. Consider finally, the phases of the sport season. Generally, early pre-season or off-season training is reserved for maximum strength and hypertrophy. For athletes new to resistance training an extended period of time may be required for functional or anatomical training - preparing the body for a more strenuous lifting program.

Strength training priorities over a season

	Priority	*Strength training goal*
Off season	High	Hypertrophy and maximal strength
Pre-season	High>>>Medium	Sport specific power and strength endurance
In-season	Medium>>>Low	Maintenance of power and strenth endurance
Transition	Low	Active rest

Step 2 - Exercise selection

Once a movement analysis of the sport has been considered and the strength objective for the program set (i.e. hypertrophy, maximum strength, power, strength endurance or a combination of several), the most appropriate exercises can be selected. Core exercises (those that incorporate one or more large muscle groups) should form the basis of a maximal strength or hypertrophy resistance training program. Examples include back squats, bench presses, dead lifts and should presses. Core exercises suitable for power development include power cleans, push jerks and snatches.

When explosive power and strength endurance are more a priority (perhaps for a late pre-season strength program) more assistance exercises can be incorporated into the routine. Assistance exercises recruit smaller muscle groups and are usually single joint exercises. They can be useful for maintaining a balance between agonists and antagonist muscle groups - especially if the sport places an uneven demand on the body. They can also closely match some of the movements in sport.

Kicking - leg extensions, hip abduction/adduction

Jumping - power cleans, calf presses, jump squats

Rowing - seated rows, hip sled, single arm rows

Swimming (front crawl) - lat pull downs, lateral raises, overhead pulls

Sprinting - lunges, step-ups, calf raises

Throwing - overhead pullovers, triceps extensions, internal/external shoulder rotations

Even though mirroring sport specific movements is an important design variable, it should not be to the neglect of other major muscle groups. A resistance training program should aim to develop balance throughout the body even if the sport has an upper or lower body emphasis. This is an important step in injury prevention. Here is an example of the exercises selected for a soccer player. After completing a series of tests, they were assessed to be lacking in power and speed, although their basic strength and strength endurance was good:

Sample exercises for a Soccer player
Core exercises

— Power cleans
— Front squats
— Bench presses
— Shoulder presses

Assistance Exercises

— Cruches
— Lat Pull Downs
— Barbell Curis
— Leg Curls
— Calf presses

Step 3 covers how this collection of resistance exercises could be organised into structured sessions to achieve the desired conditioning outcome.

Step 3 - Frequency

Fequency

Many athletes choose to lift weights in three workouts a week. This often works well allowing sufficient recovery time and fits nicely into the 7-day week. More advanced lifters may benefit from a four, five or even six day a week program.

Beginners are recommended to start with two, total body sessions a week. Guidelines from the National Strength and Conditioning Association suggest that there should be at least one rest day but not more than three between working each muscle group. At a minimum, a resistance training session that works the entire body could be completed Monday and Thursday or Tuesday and Saturday.

Alternatively, it may be more suitable to use the split routine design - training different muscle groups on different days. It's also important to take the phases of season into consideration.

— Off Season - 4-6 sessions per week
— Pre Season - 3-4 sessions per week
— In Season - 1-2 sessions per week
— Transition - 0-3 sessions per week

Of course frequency design cannot be complete without taking other elements of training into account. A resistance training program for a hockey player for example, might be coupled with plyometric training. In this scenario, only two resistance training sessions per week is feasible.

Sample split routines

Program design	*Mon*	*Tue*	*Wed*	*Thu*	*Fri*	*Sat*	*Sun*
Total Body	Total Body	Rest	Rest	Total Body	Rest	Rest	Rest
Upper/Lower body Split	Upper body	Lower body		Upper body	Lower body		
Push/pull Split	Chest Shoulders Tricpes		Legs		Back Traps Biceps		
Body part split	Chest & back	Legs	Shoulders arms	Rest	Chest& back	Legs	Shou-lders arms

Step 4 - Exercise order

The order in which exercises are performed in a session should not be overlooked. Sports conditioning is more demanding than general fitness training and with various forms of training often taking place in the week it's important to maximise overload to recovery ratio. One method for structuring exercise order is power, core, assistance exercises. So for example, power cleans (which involves the most complex movements) should start the session if they are included. A resistance training session that follows this structure might look as follows:

— Hang cleans (power)
— Back Squats (core)
— Bench Presses (core)
— Bent Over Rows (assistance)
— Triceps Push Downs (assistance)

A second approach is to alternate upper and lower body exercises:

— Lunges
— Seated rows
— Leg Curls
— Reverse Flies
— Calf Presses
– Barbell Curls

Finally, the push-pull format is an effective resistance training session structure. For the upper body:

— Incline Bench Presses
— Lat Pull Downs
— Military Presses
— Hammer Curls

And for the lower body:

— Front Squats
— Stiff Leg Deadlifts
— Hip Sleds
— Leg Curls

Sticking with the soccer training example from Step 2, here's how that selection of exercises could be structured into an Off-season weekly resistance training plan:

Off season Soccer resistance program

Mon (Lower Body)	*Tue (Upper Body)*	*Wed*	*Thu*	*Fri*
Power cleans	Bench Presses	Rrst	Upper	Lower
Front Squats	Lat Pull Downs	Body	Body	
Leg Curls	Barbell Curls			
Calf Presses	Crunches			

Notice how the sessions are split into the "upper body / lower body format" over the week. For the individual sessions exercises are ordered by a "push-pull" format.

Step 5 - Loading & repetitions

Assigning the right intensity or load to the exercises depends on two main factors the training objective and the athlete's current level of strength. Loads are usually assigned as a percentage of the athlete's one repetition maximum. The Table below shows the relationship between loading patterns and the conditioning response:

Relationship Between Load, Repetitions And Training Objective		
Training Objective	**Load (% 1RM)**	**Target Repetitions**
Strength	> 85	< 6
Power	75-85	3-5
Hypertrophy	67-85	6-12
Strength Endurance	< 67	> 12

Using the chart above, for an athlete to make the greatest gains in maximal strength they should perform sets of 6 repetitions or less. That means that failure to lift another, single repetition should occur within 6 repetitions - which typically correlates to a load of greater than 85% 1RM

Strength endurance, on the other hand, is developed when a greater number of repetitions are completed and loads usually correlate to less than 67% 1RM. It's important to remember that adequate overload, even when strength endurance is the primary objective, occurs when each set is performed to, or close to failure.

Explosive power development is a little different. From the chart above, power for multi-sprint sports (as opposed to single power events such as Olympic Weightlifting) is best developed in a repetition range of 3-5. However, if exercises were performed to failure in this repetition range, loads of approximately 87-93% 1RM would be used. This is too heavy for substantial power production as it limits the athlete's ability to generate speed of movement. Instead, the 3-5 repetitions are completed with loads of 75-85% 1RM with emphasis on the quality of the lifts.

Step 6 - Volume

Volume can be classed as the total amount of weight lifted in a resistance training session. This is calculated by multiplying the weight used for each set for all exercises by the number of repetitions completed. So if 3 sets of bench presses are completed, each for 10 repetitions, using 175lbs (80kg) the total volume load equates as:

3sets x 10reps x 175lbs = 5250lbs

Research has shown that gain in both hypertrophy and maximal strength can be achieved with a single set per exercise. However, many more studies suggest that while suitable for beginners, more advanced lifters require additional volume to make further gains in strength. It's also interesting to note that there is evidence that 3 sets of 10 repetitions completed without going to failure increase strength to a greater degree than 1 set of 10 repetitions completed to failure. As with load, volume is dependant on the athlete's previous training history and the primary strength objective. One or two sets are suitable for beginners and up to 6 sets for experienced athletes. The chart below outlines the general relationship between volume and different aspects of strength:

Relationship between volume and training objective

Training objective	*Target Repetitions*	*Sets*
Strength	<6	2-6
Power	3-5	3-5
Hypertrophy	6-12	3-6
Strength endurance	>12	2-3

Rest Periods

Maximal strength training places the greatest demands on the neuromuscular system and requires the longest rest interval between sets and should last between 2-6 minutes. Resistance training for power demands high quality of movement and the resulting fatigue from too short a rest interval compromises lifting technique. Rest periods of 2-5 minutes are also recommended for power training. Rest interval of 30 seconds to 1.5minutes are suggested for hypertrophy and les than 30 seconds for imprcvements in strength endurance.

Step 7 - Progression

From phase to phase over the course of a season, resistance training usually progresses from general strength to sport-specific power and strength endurance.

The in-season sees a reduction in training volume where the goal is to maintain the gains made in the off and pre-season phases. From session to session loads and volume should increase gradually. The 2-for-2 rule is a useful guideline for increasing the resistance. For example, 3 sets of 8 repetitions may be prescribed for a particular exercise. When the athlete completes 2 more repetitions (i.e. 10 reps) on the final set for 2 consecutive sessions the weight should be increased. For smaller muscle groups an increase of 2.5-5lbs (1.25-2.5kg) is suggested and 5-10lbs (2.5-5kg) for larger muscle groups.

Core Strength Training

Core strength training may be a relatively new, buzz term in the fitness industry but coaches and athletes have understood its value for many years. The core region consists of far more than just the abdominal muscles. In fact core strength training aims to target all the muscles groups that stabilise the spine and pelvis. It's these muscle groups that are critical for the transfer of energy from large to small body parts during many sporting activities.

Core Strength Training For Athletic Performance

The muscles of the trunk and torso act to stabilise the spine, pelvis and shoulder girdle. From this solid, balanced base the limbs can be moved powerfully and under control. In fact before rapid movements of the extremities can take place, the central nervous system stabilises the spine in anticipation. The rate at which the core muscles stabilise the spine may have a direct effect on the power of limb movement.

Core strength training differs from many traditional weight training routines by working both the lower back and abdominals in unison. The same is true for the upper and lower body. All athletic movements incorporate the core in some way. Very few muscle groups are isolated. Instead the whole body works as a unit and core strength training endeavours to replicate this. What are the benefits of core strength training to the athlete?

— Greater efficiency of movement
— Improved body control and balance
— Increased power output from both the core musculature and peripheral muscles such as the shoulders, arms and legs
— Reduced risk of injury (the core muscles act as shock absorbers for jumps and rebounds etc.)
— Improved balance and stability
— Improved athletic performance!

Core Strength Training for Reducing Back Problems

Weak or poorly controlled core muscles have been associated with low back pain. The back muscles are responsible for movements such as extension and flexion of the spine and rotation of the trunk.

Excessive or uneven shock on the spine may lead to back problems. This may be exaggerated because weak core muscles lead to improper positioning or a forward tilt. In many exercises that use the back muscles, the abdominal muscles contract isometrically stabilising the body.

The stronger and more correctly balanced the core muscles are, the less the uneven strain on the spine.

Equipment Used For Core Strength Training

While there are no doubt countless gimmicks on the market purporting to strengthen the core region most are useless to the athlete. There are however, several pieces of exercise equipment that are genuinely useful for strengthening the core region. They include:

- Medicine Balls
- Stability Balls
- Balance Boards

These simple pieces of equipment allow the coach or athlete to devise resisted sport-specific movements. Medicine balls are particular helpful for mimicking rotation movements for example that would be unpractical with free weights. Of course even these pieces of equipment are not essential. There are many exercises that use bodyweight or partner resistance that strengthen the core effectively. The use of free weights can adapted to cater for the majority of athletic movements.

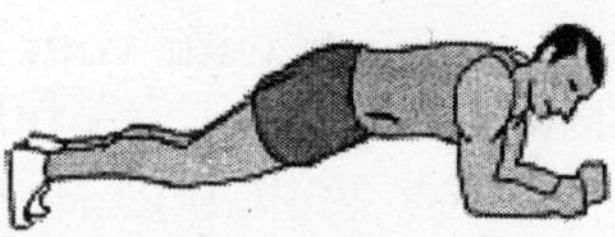

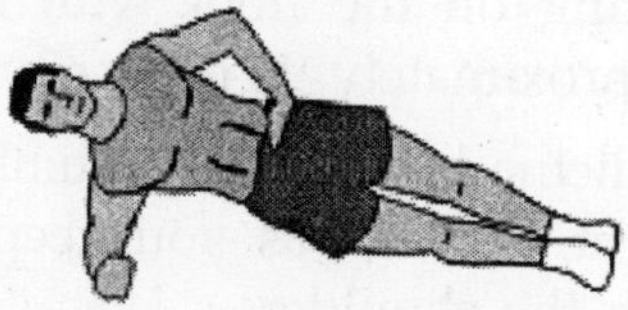

Popular Core Strength Training Exercises

Prone bridge

In a face down position, balance on the tips of your toes and elbows while attempting to maintain a straight line from heels to head. This exercise focuses on both the anterior and posterior muscle groups of the trunk and pelvis.

Lateral bridge

Start on your side and press up with your right arm. Form a bridge maintaining a straight line from your hand to your foot. Rest on your elbow to increase the difficulty. This exercise focuses on the abdominal obliques and transversus abdominus

Supine bridge

Lying on your back, raise your hips so that only your head, shoulders, and feet are touching the floor. The supine bridge focuses on the gluteal muscles. Stronger gluteals help maintain pelvic control

Pelvic thrusts

Lie on your back with your legs bent 90 degrees at the hip. Slowly lift your hips off the floor and towards the ceiling. Lower your hips to the floor and repeat for the prescribed number of repetitions.

Russian twists

1. Start by sitting on the floor with hips and knees flexed to approximately 90 degree angles.
2. Grasp a medicine ball or small dumbbell and swing it to the right and left as you keep the hips from rotating with the shoulders.
3. The arms are not perpendicular to the torso, but instead, kept low, near the thighs, as the medicine ball is swung to each side.

Good mornings

1) Stand with feet shoulder width apart with knees slightly bent (at 20°).

2) Start position: Grasp bar with overhand grip shoulder width apart. Back should be straight in a neutral position.

3) Bending at the hips, lower bar to approximately knee height. Keep knees bent at 20° throughout movement.

4) Return to start position.

5) Remember to keep back straight - movement should occur at the hip. To facilitate this, shift glutes back as if ready to sit down. Knees should not move forward beyond the toes.

Dumbell lunges with crossover

1) Start position: Stand with feet hip width apart. Grasp DB's and hold out in front of body.

2) Step forward 2-3 feet forming a 90° bend at the front hip and knee. DO NOT allow front knee to extend past the big toe - may cause injury. As you are lunging swing dumbbells across body towards the hip.

3) Pushing off front foot, return to start position with legs and dumbbells.

4) Remember to keep head and back upright in a neutral position. Shoulders and hips should remain squared at all times.

5) Watch for proper knee alignment - do not let front knee extend past big toe or deviate laterally or medially. Back knee should not come in contact with floor.

Other excellent core stability exercises include:

— Lat Pull Downs

— Leg Presses/Squats

— Crunches and crunch variations
— Regular lunges
— Back extensions
— Deadlifts
— Chin-ups

Resistance Band Exercises

Resistance band exercises are widely used by a variety of health and fitness practitioners - both for general strength and conditioning and rehabilitation or injury prevention. Resistance band exercises are ideal for home exercise programs and can easily be incorporated into a circuit training format helping to condition cardiovascular system as well as strengthening specific muscle groups. Because resistance tubing is so compact and lightweight, it can be used while away from home.

Resistance tubing is extremely adaptable and a large number of resistance band exercises can be developed with very little additional equipment. Smaller muscle groups that are hard to train with more traditional free weight exercises can be targeted with resistance tubing. This makes it particularly appealing to athletic conditioning.

Sports-specific conditioning involves training movements rather than individual muscle groups. The versatility of resistance band exercises allows the athlete to mirror very closely the movement patterns in their sport with varying degrees of resistance. Perhaps even more important is the role they can play in injury prevention and rehabilitation.

Resistance Band Exercises for Injury Prevention & Rehabilitation

Few studies have examined the effects of resistance band exercises on strengthening a specific muscle group. As a result no definite guidelines exist as to the number of sets, repetitions and amount of resistance that should be used. However, many health and fitness practitioners use resistance tubing routinely to prevent and rehabilitate overuse injuries by strengthening often smaller, neglected muscle groups.

For example, athletic movements such as a baseball pitch can place considerable demand on the posterior rotator cuff muscles (external rotators, supraspinatus, infraspinatus, teres minor). These muscles undergo eccentric contraction during the declaration phase of the pitch, which places considerable strain on the shoulder. However, the same muscles may not be effectively worked with traditional isotonic exercises. If larger muscle groups, such as the deltoids, become stronger and are able to cope with and apply greater force, this may further compromise the rotator cuff muscles.

A program of resistance band exercises to compliment regular strength training may be able to improve the strength of more isolated muscle groups such as the rotator cuff. Additionally, training these otherwise neglected muscles may even improve performance.

Resistance Band Exercises

Of course resistance band exercises can be used for more than simply strengthening more isolated muscle groups. The exercises below work the major muscle groups are only a small sample of the many hundreds of variations that have been devised.

Athletes may want to incorporate them into an off season training program when recovery and regeneration is the most important goal. Resistance bands are available in a range of colors that relate to their stiffness or resistance. Color-coding varies between the brands but it typically as follows:

— Yellow (thin)
— Red (medium)
— Green (heavy)
— Blue (extra heavy)
— Black (special heavy)
— Silver (super heavy)

For the resistance band exercises below, complete 2-3 sets of 12-15 repetitions. You should warm up first with 5-10 minutes of light aerobic exercise and cool down with another 5-10 minutes of gentle exercise, plus some stretching exercises.

Resistance band squats

1. Start by stepping on the resistance band with both feet shoulder width apart.
2. Hold the resistance band at shoulder level with both hands. Start into a full squat while holding the band at shoulder height.
3. Return to the starting position and repeat.

Resistance band bent over rows

1. Start by placing the band under one foot and stepping backwards with the other foot.
2. Bend over keeping your back flat and stop at a 45 degree angle.
3. Pull the bands up towards your waist keeping your elbows in close together.
4. Squeeze your shoulder blades together when performing rowing motion.

Alternate lying chest presses

1. Lie on your back and place the resistance band under your back and hold the ends with both hands.

2. Start by pressing one arm up towards the ceiling and then return to the starting position. Repeat with the other arm.

Diagonal woodchops

Starting Position: Loop the band under your left foot and grasp either end. Keep hands together and extend arms down towards left foot.

1. Bring band up and away in a wood chopping motion.
2. During this motion your feet stay stationary and you rotate at your trunk. Repeat this motion for the desired repetitions and then repeat in the opposite direction.

Triceps extension with resistance band

1. Start by holding the tubing in one hand and placing that hand behind your back.
2. Now grab the other end of the band with the arm that is over your head.
3. Extend the top elbow until your arm is fully extended.
4. Return to the starting position and repeat for the prescribed repetitions.

Resistance band lunges

1. Stand with feet hip width apart. Take left leg and step back approximately 2 feet standing on the ball of the foot. Place resistance band under front foot and hold the other end with your hands.
2. Start position: Feet should be positioned at a staggered stance with head and back erect and straight in a neutral position.

3. Lower body by bending at right hip and knee until thigh is parallel to floor. Body should follow a straight line down towards the floor.
4. Return to start position.

Lateral rows with resistance band

1. Step onto resistance band with feet hip width apart and knees slightly bent.
2. Start position: Grasp ends with a neutral grip (palms facing each other). Arms should hang down to sides with elbows slightly bent.
3. Raise band to side of body at shoulder height keeping elbows only slightly bent.
4. Return to start position.

Biceps curls with eesistance band

1. Stand with feet shoulder width apart, knees slightly bent, and at a staggered stance.
2. Step onto middle of tubing with back foot or both feet.
3. Start position: Grasp ends with underhand grip (palms facing forward) with arms hanging down at sides. Elbows should be close to sides.
4. Flex at the elbows and curl band up to approximately shoulder level. Keep elbows close to sides throughout movement. 5. Return to start position.
6. Remember to keep back and head straight in a neutral position throughout movement. Shoulders should be stabilised by squeezing shoulder blades together slightly - only the elbow joint should be moving.

Kettlebell Exercises

Here are the kettlebell exercises and images. If you missed the kettleball training article you can see an example of how these exercises can make up a routine. Do kettlebell exercises offer any performance advantages over regular freeweights and dumbbells? Not necessarily. An athlete must be very selective over the training they choose to integrate into their program. They have a limited amount of time and energy and each element of conditioning must take the whole into account. Unless you are a Girevik, think seriously before replacing proven training methods for kettlebell routines.

Kettlebell exercises

It goes without saying that should perform a throrough warm up before any exercise session. And with these kettlebell exercises it's doubly important. Do 5-10 minutes of light aerobic activity followed by stretching exercises to all the major muscle groups.

Kettlebell cleans

1. Keep torso straight but bent forward at the hips slightly.
2. Explosively raise the kettleballs by extending the hips, knee and ankle in a "jumping action".
3. Keep your elbows out and shoulders directly above the kettleballs as long as possible. Keep the kettleballs close to the body.
4. Once you have extended the lower leg shrug your shoulders and at maximum elevation of the shoulders start pulling with the arms. Keep the elbows high during the pull until the highest point.
5. Rotate elbows around and underneath the kettleballs. Rack your hands across the front of the

shoulders. Slightly flex the hips and knees to absorb the weight.

6. This should be a fluid motion where all the steps flow together.

Single Arm Kettlebell Row

1. Stand with feet hip width and knees slightly bent. Bend at hips with back straight and knees bent.
2. Take one hand and place on stationary object that is approximately waist height to support upper body.
3. Hold kettleball in other hand with a neutral grip and let arm hang straight down (perpendicular to floor).
4. Keeping elbows close to body, pull kettleball up to body and squeeze shoulder blades together at top of movement.
5. Return to start position. Remember to keep back and head straight - hyperextension, flexion, or trunk rotation may cause injury.

Alternating floor press

1. Lie on your back holding a kettleball in each hand.
2. Alternating with your arms push up one kettleball at a time.
3. Slightly rotate your trunk when pressing the kettleball up. Repeat with the other arm.

Kettlebell front squat

1. Grasp kettleballs and hold them at chest level in front of you.
2. Stand with feet slightly wider than hip width apart. Knees should be slightly bent.
3. Lower body by flexing at the hips and knees. Upper body can flex forward at the hips slightly (~5°)

during movement. Be sure to "sit back" so that knees stay over the feet.

4. Once thighs are parallel to floor, return to start position.

Single arm Kettlebell Jerk

1. Stand with feet shoulder width apart and knees slightly bent. Position kettleball to ear level with an overhand grip (palms facing forward).
2. Go into a quick ¼ squat. Immediately extend legs and stand up and at the same time press hands up above head keeping wrists over the elbow and arm moving parallel to body at all times.
3. Return to start position. This is an explosive exercise and the legs are used to be able to lift more weight overhead

Kettlebell swing

1. Hold one kettleball between your legs and your body is in a bentover stance with your back flat.
2. Swing the kettleball backwards and then forcefully swing the kettleball forward to a chest level. Keep your arm straight and forcefully extend your hips, knees, and ankles.

Kettlebell windmill

1. Place one arm overhead full extended with a kettleball. Bend forward at the hips keeping back flat to grab the other kettleball with the free hand.
2. While holding one kettleball overhead continue to raise and lower the other kettleball.
3. Continue for the desired repetitions and repeat with the other arm.

There are literally dozens of kettlebell exercises you can perform. Just as with other free weights, the combinations and variations are endless. However, athletes should remember the principle of specificity. Pick kettlebell exercises that most closely match the movement patterns of your sport.

Kettlebell exercises may not be as effective as more traditional free weights for developing maximal strength - an important phase in the athlete's overall program. The movement patterns and loads they incorporate makes them better suited to converting maximal strength into explosive power and / or strength endurance.

A Full-Body Kettlebell Training Program for Strength, Power and Endurance

Kettlebell training is rapidly growing in popularity amongst general fitness enthusiasts and athletes. Used by the Russian military and Special Forces, the kettlebell (or girya) has been touted as the most effective, efficient piece of strength training equipment available. Proponents of kettlebell training suggest that it increases strength, power, speed, co-ordination as well as core stability. Some even claim that it can replace several different forms of training and is superior to more traditional weight training.

A commonly cited study by Voropayev in 1983 is used as evidence that kettlebell training is more effective than traditional training. In this study two groups of college students were followed over several years. One group followed a standard military regimen of pull-ups, 100m sprints, standing broad jumps, and a 1km run.

The experimental group used nothing but kettlebells and kettlebell exercises. Both groups were then tested using the same military exercises. The kettlebell group scored higher in every test - including those that were not purely strength based. So could kettlebell training be a 'magic bullet' for athletes?

Kettlebell Training for Sport-Specific Conditioning

From an athlete's perspective, the most important principle to remember is specificity. Exercises and intensity should mirror the demands of the sport. That may be best achieved through the use of dumbbells, medicine balls, resistance machines OR kettlebells. But an athlete should think seriously about basing their strength training entirely around just a few kettlebell exercises.

Girevoy Sport (a Russian-born competition using exclusively kettlebells) is not just about strength - Gireviks require tremendous strength endurance. As a result, kettlebells are lighter than you might think. A 35lb (16kg) kettlebell can provide a very demanding workout even for an extremely fit male. A 53-pound (24kg) kettlebell is considered heavy and lighter weights include 26lb (12kg), 18lb (8kg) and 9lb (4kg).

So traditional kettlebell training is not about lifting maximum loads. In this sense, it won't lead to the same neural adaptations as maximal strength training with traditional free weights. Maximal strength training is an important phase in most sport-specific strength programs. It allows potentially greater development of explosive power and / or strength endurance in later phases.

Kettlebell training may be more useful for a phase of explosive power training. One method used for developing power is through plyometrics. However, this is not the only way to convert gain in maximal strength into sport-specific power. The use of lighter resistances and increased speed of muscle contraction may mean that some kettlebell exercises are highly suited to relevant sports.

Kettlebell Training During the Off-Season

The off season is usually a good time to spend on more functional-type strength training. It not only provides respite from very intense maximal strength and power training, but can also be used to restore any imbalances between opposing muscle groups for example.

Many kettlebell exercises work all the major muscle groups simultaneously. In this respect they can help to restore some of the physical imbalances that are inherent in many athletes.

However, remember that the off-season is primarily about recovery. Some kettlebell routines are gruelling to say the least so choose exercises, load and particularly volume very carefully. Below is a sample routine using only kettlebells. Athletes may want to cherry-pick some of the exercises for in-season training. Alternatively, the routine could be used as is during the off-season.

Sample Kettlebell Training Routine

Below is a sample routine using only kettlebells. Athletes may want to cherry-pick some of the exercises for in-season training. Alternatively, the routine could be used as is during the off-season.

— Power Cleans - 3 sets x 15-20 reps

— Single Arm Rows - 3 sets x 15-20 reps

— Alternating Floor Press - 3 sets x 15-20 reps

— Front Squat - 3 sets x 15-20 reps

— Single Arm Jerk - 3 sets x 15-20 reps

— Kettlebell Swing - 3 sets x 15-20 reps

— Kettlebell Windmill - 3 sets x 15-20 reps

Medicine Ball Exercises

Medicine ball exercises are an important tool for

developing sport-specific power. They can be used as part of a circuit training format or plyometrics program. In fact, upper body plyometric exercises are limited without their use.

Strength training for sport, for the most part, is very different from bodybuilding. While a phase of the strength training program should focus on maximal strength development and occasionally hypertrophy, it is explosive power and/or strength endurance that should be the end-goal for most athletes. While there are various methods to increase power, a common element is speed of contraction. Medicine balls are relatively light allowing exercises to be performed explosively.

Medicine ball exercises allow the athlete and coach to devise drills that closely match the movements within a particular sport. Take tennis training for example. Mirroring the movement patterns of a forehand or backhand stroke with traditional free weights is difficult. Torso twists, where the ball is released to a partner incorporate many of the same muscle groups in the same firing pattern as a tennis forehand or backhand stroke. And of course medicine ball exercises are not limited to tennis. They have obvious application to sports such as:

— Athletics (field events)

— Baseball

— Basketball

— Football

— Netball

— Rugby

— Squash and Racket ball

— Soccer (goalkeepers)

— Volleyball

Incorporating Medicine Ball Exercises into a Program

Medicine ball exercises have their place in an overall strength program. That doesn't mean to say they should replace all forms of strength training however. Rather than following a medicine ball 'routine' as such, a more appropriate approach is to select a few exercises and incorporate them into a circuit or session designed to increase power and/or strength endurance.

Remember also, that medicine ball exercises are effective and should only be selected if the closely mirror the movements within the sport. Athletes spend a great deal of time and energy training and all exercises should be chosen with care to ensure they make the very most if the training time available.

The very best to incorporate medicine ball exercises into the overall conditioning program is to use the principle of periodisation. By splitting the annual strength program into several phases, different elements of strength can be developed that will enhance the next phase of training. Medicine ball exercises used to develop explosive power will be more effective if they are performed after a phase of maximal strength training. The idea is that the more strength you have to work with, the more of it you can convert into sport-specific power.

General guidelines

— Warm up thoroughly before starting a medicine ball routine.

— Ensure you have plenty of space and a competent training partner when performing these drills.

— Medicine ball exercises, as with other forms of power training, should be completed when you are fresh before heavy aerobic or anaerobic training if completed in the same day.

— Focus on speed of movement but not at the sacrifice of technique.

— Do not choose a ball that is so heavy it slows the movement of the exercise down.

— Complete 1-3 sets of 8-10 repetitions for each exercise.

— When standing and throwing from behind the head, be careful not to hyperextend the spine too far.

Sample Medicine Ball Exercises

Kneel to push ups

1. Start Position: Your body will be in an upright position sitting on your knees.
2. Hold medicine ball at chest level. Keeping your torso erect fall forward and chest press the medicine ball to a partner or a wall.
3. Upon releasing the ball drop your hands to the floor and immediately complete a push-up.
4. Advanced athletes: To make this more challenging have a partner throw the ball back to you. You will have to explode up with the push-up so that you are back in the seated upright position on your knees. Your partner will throw the ball back to you and then repeat the exercise until the desired repetitions are met.

Single leg chops

1. Starting Position: Stand on right leg and your arms are extended holding the medicine ball up and to your right.
2. Bring medicine ball down in a wood chopping motion towards your left foot.

3. During this place motion switch feet so your left foot is now on the ground and your right foot is in the air. Repeat this motion for the desired repetitions and then repeat in the opposite direction.

Slams

1. Stand with feet parallel and knees slightly bent.
2. Pull medicine ball back behind head and forcefully throw ball down on the ground as hard as possible.
3. Catch the ball on the bounce from the ground and repeat according to prescribed repetitions.

Figure of eights

1. Start Position: Hold medicine ball with your arms extended over your right shoulder.
2. In one continuous motion bring the ball down in front of you like you are chopping wood and the ball should end towards your left foot.
3. Stand back up and raise the ball straight up over your left shoulder and now bring the ball down towards your right foot.
4. You will have to bend at your knees to complete this.
5. Return to starting position and repeat.

Medicine Ball Lunge Crossovers

1. Stand with feet hip width apart. Take left leg and step back approximately 2 feet standing on the ball of the foot.
2. Start position: Feet should be positioned at a staggered stance with head and back erect and straight in a neutral position. Hold medicine ball in front of your chest.

3. Lower body by bending at hip and knee until thigh is parallel to floor. Body should follow a straight line down towards the floor. As you are lunging reach to one side of the leg with the ball.
4. Return to start position and repeat by reaching to the opposite side with the ball. Alternate or switch to other leg after prescribed reps.

Russian twists

1. Stand with feet hip-width apart.
2. Hold medicine ball with both hands and arms only slightly bent.

3. Swing ball over to the right hip and forcefully swing ball forward and around towards the left side. Reverse back in the opposite direction. Keep the stomach drawn in to maximise proper usage of muscle.

Single Leg V-Ups

1. Start position: Lie back onto floor or bench with knees bent, both hands behind head. Keep elbow back and out of sight. Head should be in a neutral position with a space between chin and chest.
2. Leading with the chin and chest towards the ceiling, contract the abdominal and raise shoulders off floor or bench. Extend arms and also raise one leg up toward ceiling.
3. Return to start position.
4. Remember to keep head and back in a neutral position. Hyperextension or flexion may cause injury. To increase resistance, hold medicine ball in hands. To decrease resistance, position hand closer towards body

Medicine Ball Obliques

1. Starting Position: Lie on your back and raise your legs with your knees bent.
2. Holding a medicine ball between your knees rotate your legs to the side and then return to the starting position. Repeat to the other side.

Lateral Flexion w/ Stability Ball

1. Starting Position: Lie on your side over the stability ball and spread your legs for balance.
2. Hold a medicine ball over your head and curl up towards the ceiling. Lay back down across the ball and repeat the movement.
3. Repeat with the other side.

Reverse Curls

1. Start position: Lie with back on floor or bench with hips flexed at 90° and feet in air holding onto a medicine ball. Position arms at sides with palms down on floor.
2. Leading with the heels towards the ceiling, raise glutes (butt) off floor or bench.
3. Return to start position.
4. Remember keep legs from swinging to prevent momentum throughout the exercise.

Stability Ball Exercises for Core Strength

Stability ball exercises are often central to a program designed to improve core stability. In recent years, health and fitness practitioners have given greater and greater emphasis to core stability training for injury prevention, rehabilitation and performance enhancement.

The concept of developing strong muscles in the trunk is believed to reduce the risk of both acute and chronic injury and weak core muscles have been associated with low back pain. Core stability can also improve athletic performance as rapid and controlled limb movement is directly related to the ability of the core muscles to stabilise the spine.

Stability ball exercises also known as Swiss ball exercises, are believed to activate the trunk musculature to a greater extent than more traditional resistance exercises. The unstable surface of the ball is thought to provide a greater challenge to the core muscles than a solid bench or standing on a stable surface. But is this the case?

Is there any evidence to suggest stability ball exercises activate the trunk muscles any more than traditional resistance exercises?

Research to suggest that this is the case is sparse. One study found that during biceps curls the activity in the rectus abdominis and external obliques increased. Another study concluded that 5 weeks of Swiss ball core stability and balance exercises increased torso balance and EMG activity compared to conventional floor exercises in women.

Other studies have established that only some of the core muscles (i.e. the rectus abdominis) are activated to a greater extent during stability ball exercises and that not all stability ball exercises induce this increased muscle activation. Additionally, researchers have questioned the value of any increased activation of the rectus abdominis, as core stability training aims to minimise its activation in favor of other surrounding muscle groups.

Several studies have shown that while stability ball exercises may improve core stability they are not necessarily any superior to conventional exercises. Of importance to athletes is that stability ball exercises may reduce maximum force production. The decreased balance associated with resistance training on an unstable surface may force the limbs (and not the core) to play a greater role in joint stability. It would be unwise for athletes to replace all resistance training on stable surfaces with stability ball exercises.

In conclusion then, there is little scientific support to suggest that stability ball exercises are superior to conventional strength training when it comes to core stability. However they do seem to improve core strength and they offer some decided advantages over traditional free weights.

Sample stability ball programs

Regardless of whether stability ball exercises are superior to other forms of resistance training or not, there is no doubt that they are extremely versatile. Stability balls lend themselves very well to home exercise programs where they can replace more cumbersome, space-consuming benches and racks. In fact with just a single stability ball, a small set of dumbbells and / or resistance bands, hundreds of very effective training programs can be completed at home.

The following stability ball exercises cover the major muscle groups of the body. They are not designed to be used with very heavy weights but with strict form and when performed with a slow, even tempo, overload can be achieved within 15-20 repetitions. They can be completed in order, for two to three sessions per week.

Athletes may benefit from stability ball exercises during off season training. The priority during the off season or transition phase is recovery and regeneration. However, the emphasis should be on active recovery rather than complete rest. Developing good core stability during this time will prepare the body for more intense resistance training later on.

Sample Stability Ball Exercises

Incline Dumbbell Chest Press

1. Lie on the ball so that the ball is under your upper back. Drop your hips so that they are only a couple of inches off the floor.
2. Start with the dumbbells at shoulder level and proceed to press them straight up toward the ceiling.
3. Remember to keep your hands directly above your elbows during the press phase. The dumbbells should end up directly above your chest.
4. Return to the starting position and repeat.
5. Complete 2 sets of 12-15 repetitions.

Squat and Press with Stability Ball

1. Stand with feet shoulder width apart and knees slightly bent.
2. Start position: Position medicine ball to ear level.
3. Go into a full squat. Immediately extend legs and stand up and at the same time press hands up above head keeping wrists over the elbows and arms moving parallel to body at all times.
4. Return to start position and repeat.
5. Complete 2 sets of 20 repetitions.

Stability Ball Crunch

1. Sit in upright position on stability ball with feet flat on floor.
2. Walk feet forward allowing stability ball to roll underneath body until it is positioned on lower to

mid-back region. Raise hips slightly to create a "table top" position parallel to floor.

3. Place hands across your chest. Head should be in a neutral position with a space between chin and chest.
4. Leading with the chin and chest towards the ceiling, contract the abdominal and raise shoulders up.
5. Return to start position.
6. Remember to keep head and back in a neutral position. Hyperextension or flexion of either may cause injury.
7. Complete 3 sets of 20 repetitions.

Dumbbell Bent Over Row with Stability Ball

1. Stand with feet hip width and knees slightly bent.
2. Start position: Bend at hips with back straight and knees bent . Take one hand and place on ball that is approximately waist height to support upper body. Hold DB in other hand with a neutral grip and let arm hang straight down (perpendicular to floor).
3. Keeping elbows close to body, pull DB up to body and squeeze shoulder blades together at top of movement.
4. Return to start position.
5. Remember to keep back and head straight - hyperextension, flexion, or trunk rotation may cause injury.
6. Complete 2 sets of 12-15 repetitions.

Shoulder Press

1. Sit in upright position on a ball.
2. Start position: Position DB's to ear level with an overhand grip (palms facing forward).

3. Press hands up above head keeping wrists over the elbows and arms moving parallel to body at all times.
4. Return to start position.
5. Remember to keep back and head straight in a neutral position - hyperextension or excessive flexion may cause injury.
6. Complete 2 sets of 12-15 repetitions.

Low Back Extension

1. Lie face down on stability ball with knees and feet on floor.
2. Stability ball placement should be at abdominal to lower chest region.
3. With hands on chest, raise trunk 4-8 inches.
4. Lower to start position.
5. To increase intensity, position ball down towards hips, feet wide with knees off floor. Hands may be placed behind head and overhead to further increase resistance. To increase stability, place feet against wall or stationary object.
6. Complete 2 sets of 12-15 repetitions.

Abdominal Exercises

Abdominal exercises play an integral role in any strength and conditioning program. A strong core is essential for athletic performance and to prevent the occurrence of injuries and back pain.

There are literally thousands of abdominal exercises and many more variations of each of them. There also innumerable fitness gimmicks promising "washboard abs" in just a few minutes exercise a day. While these exercise aids may or may not be effective at strengthening the core they are unnecessary. Plenty of abdominal exercises that require nothing other than an exercise mat or towel will strengthen the muscles of the core region just as effectively. The abdominal exercises below have been spit into three groups - basic advanced and sport-specific.

Basic Abdominal Exercises

Basic strength in the stomach can be developed with following abdominal exercises. Start by aiming for 1-3 sets of 10 repetitions three times per week and gradually build up to 20-25 repetitions.

Static Contraction

1) Lying flat on your back bend your knees bent so feet are flat on the floor.
2) Contract your stomach muscles and try to push the small of your back into the floor.
3) Hold for a count of 5 seconds remembering to breathe gently. Relax and repeat for the desired number of repetitions.

Keep your neck and face relaxed. Many people have a tendency to hold their breath during this exercise which can increase blood pressure.

Wrist ups

1) Lying flat on your back bend your knees to right angles keeping your feet flat on the floor.
2) Place your palms on your thighs and sit up until your fingertips reach your knees as you breathe out. Return to the start position and repeat for the desired number of repetitions.

Imagine you have an apple under your chin. That's about the distance your chin should stay away from your chest during the movement.

Oblique crunches

Abdominal exercises such as these emphasize the internal and external obliques rather than the rectuse abdominus and transverse abdominus.

1) Lie flat on your back, knees bent at right angles and twisted to the left.
2) Place your fingertips to the side of your head just behind your ears.
3) Curl up just enough to lift both your shoulders off the floor a few inches.
4) Hold that position contracting your abs as forcefully as possible as breathe out.
5) Repeat for the desired number of reps before to switching to the other side.

Supermans

This is not technically an abdominally exercise at it works the lower back.

1) Lie on your front with arms outstretched over your head, palms on the floor.
2) Simultaneously raise your right arm and left leg off the floor about 6 inches keeping them extended.
3) Hold for 5 seconds and repeat with the opposite arm and leg.
4) Repeat for the desired number of repetitions.

Advanced abdominal exercises

Once you can comfortably perform the basic abdominal exercises above try the more advanced exercises. Again start by aiming for 2-3 sets of 10-12 repetitions and progress to 20-25 repetitions per set.

Double crunches

1) Lie back onto floor or bench with knees bent and hands behind head. Keep elbows back and out of sight. Head should be in a neutral position with a space between chin and chest.
2) Start position: Hands behind head and knees bent at 90 degrees.
3. Leading with the chin and chest towards the ceiling, contract the abdominals and raise shoulders off floor or bench. During the crunch, also bring knees towards chest.
4) Return to start position and repeat.
5) Remember to keep head and back in a neutral position. Hyperextension or flexion of either may cause injury.

Side bridge

Start on your right side and press up with your right arm. Form a bridge with your arm extended and hold for 10 seconds rather than performing 10 repetitions. Gradually build up to 30 seconds plus and repeat for 2-3 sets.

V-Ups

1) Start position: Lie back onto floor or bench with knees bent and hands extended towards ceiling. Head should be in a neutral position with a space between chin and chest.
2) Leading with the chin and chest towards the ceiling, contract the abdominal and raise shoulders off floor or bench. Also raise legs up towards ceiling and attempt to touch your hands to your feet.
3) Return to start position and repeat.

Plank supermans

Starting Position: Start the movement in a plank position. Holding that position raise your right arm and left leg off of the ground. Return to the starting position and repeat with the other arm and leg. Hold each lift for 1-2 seconds and repeat for the desired number or repetitions.

Sport Specific Abdominal Exercises

The muscles of the core region are important in many athletic movements. By acting to stabilise the pelvis and spine they allow more rapid and powerful movements of the limbs. Core stability can also reduce the risk of both acute and chronic injuries.

It's worth bearing in mind that core stability is not simply a case of strengthening the stomach muscles. While abdominal exercises certainly have their place in sport-specific strength training programs, various types of resistance exercises are important to strengthen other core muscles. Remember also that if performed correctly, compound exercises involving multiple joints will often work the abdominals as they contract isometrically to stabilise the trunk.

Few if any abdominal exercises are suitable for all sports. A needs analysis of the athlete and movement analysis of their sport will confirm which abdominal exercises are most appropriate. The following exercises will help to develop basic strength in the abdominals and prepare the core region for more explosive and demanding exercises later on:

Basic Crunch / Sit Up

This is abdominal exercise can be used by a wide variety of athletes to build basic strength in the abdominal muscles. Variations include:

— Twisting during the sit up to touch either knee with each eblow
— Holding the end position for several seconds
— V-ups or doubles crunches
— Sitting up to catch or head a ball

Medicine ball plank

1) On your knees and place hands on a medicine ball.
2) Start position: Align hands at nipple line, place feet hip width apart on toes, and extend the arms to raise body up. Trunk and hips should be in a straight line.
3) Hold for 10 seconds. This is one set. Gradually build up to 30 seconds plus.

The following exercises replicate and help to improve the many athletic movements involve twisting and turning:

Seated Russian Twists

1) Sitting down suspend your feet off of the ground.
2) Holding a medicine ball rotate your shoulders side to side touching the medicine ball to the ground. Keep feet off floor
3) Repeat for the prescribed number of repetitions.

Side Throws

1) Stand with feet hip-width apart; place left foot approximately one foot in front of right foot.
2) Hold medicine ball with both hands and arms only slightly bent.
3) Swing ball over to the right hip and forcefully underhand toss ball forward to a partner or wall. Keep the stomach drawn in to maximise proper usage of muscle.

4) Catch ball on the bounce from your partner or wall and repeat according to prescribed repetitions.

Explosive power is essential in many sports. These abdominal exercises will help to develop power in the core musculature:

Slams

1) Stand with feet parallel and knees slightly bent.
2) Pull medicine ball back behind head and forcefully throw ball down on the ground as hard as possible.
3) Catch the ball on the bounce from the ground and repeat according to prescribed repetitions.

Single Arm Throws

1) Stand with feet slightly wider than hip-width apart.
2) Grasp medicine ball and lower body into a semi-squat position. Explode up extending the entire body and throwing the ball up into the air.
3) The goal is to throw the ball as high as you can and generating most of the power in the legs. Minimise the time between squatting down and exploding up i.e. don't stay in a crouched position.
4) Catch ball on the bounce and repeat according to prescribed repetitions.

Isometric Exercises & Static Strength Training

Isometric exercises, also known as static strength training, involve muscular actions in which the length of the muscle does not change and there is no visible movement at the joint. The term 'static contraction training' is sometimes used to describe isometrics. However, 'contraction' signifies a change in length (shortening) of the muscle belly, which does not occur during static strength training. The term 'static action' is preferred to static contraction.

Isometric exercises can be used for general strength conditioning and for rehabilitation where strengthening the muscles without placing undue stress on the joint is warranted. Some actions within a wide variety of sports require isometric or static strength. Examples include climbing, mountain biking and motocross (grip and upper body strength), Judo,· wrestling, alpine skiing (static strength required to stabilise the upper and lower body), shooting, gymnastics and horseback riding.

Isometric exercises can be completed with submaximal muscle action - such as holding a weight steady, out to the side. The force used to hold the weight still is not maximal as this would lift the weight further causing movement and a change in the muscle length and joint angle. Static strength training can also involve maximal muscle actions and examples here include pushing against an immoveable object such as a wall or heavy weight.

Both submaximal and maximal isometric muscle actions can increase isometric strength and induce muscular hypertrophy. In practice, maximal isometric exercises are used for strength and conditioning and submaximal exercises are used for rehabilitation.

Although isometric exercises can increase strength they are not the most suitable form of resistance training for dynamic actions such as sprinting and jumping. Most sports and athletic movements are dynamic in nature, performed at maximal speed against little or no external resistance. Isometric exercises do not increase the limb's maximal velocity and only strengthen the muscle at the angle at which it is trained.

Guidelines For Isometric Exercises

Isometric exercises can raise blood pressure significantly for the duration of the exercise. While it will return to a resting level soon after, this can be dangerous for people with hypertension or any form of cardiovascular disease. Even if you don't suffer from high blood pressure it is important to breath continuously throughout the exercises. Breath holding will only compound any increases in blood pressure.

As with all forms of exercise you should warm up thoroughly first. Muscles are under tension for a longer period of time and although that tension is more constant compared to a dynamic contraction, tears can still occur. Finally, try to maintain some degree of tension in the abdominal region during all exercises. This will help to maintain a correct posture and will help to develop core stability.

Number & Duration of Muscle Actions

Volume for a classic strength training routine is prescribed based on the number of sets and repetitions. The equivalent in isometric exercises is the length of time each action is held for and the number actions in total. Research has measured both longer duration actions (i.e. 10 seconds or above) and fewer repetitions, and shorter duration actions (i.e. 2-3 seconds) with more repetitions. Both approaches seem to increase static strength.

The general consensus is that in healthy individuals training to improve strength (as opposed to rehabilitation of an injury), the most efficient use of isometric exercises is 15-20 maximal voluntary actions held for 3 to 5 seconds. Three sessions per week is required and results can be seen in as little as 2 weeks. However, when submaximal loads are used (such as bodyweight) it may be more suitable to increase the duration and reduce the number of repetitions.

This number and duration of contractions is required for each muscle group. As with traditional dynamic strength training, exercise selection should be based on a needs analysis of the athlete. Multi joint isometric exercises such as static leg presses may be more suitable then isolating the quadriceps, hamstrings and other hip flexors / extensors.

Joint angles

Isometric exercises strengthen the muscle at or near to the joint angle at which the exercise is performed. For example a static bicep exercise held with the joint at 25° only increases the athlete's strength at that specific angle and there is no gain in strength when the elbow is held at other angles. However, at particular joint angles there is some cross-transference of strength to other joint angles. An isometric bicep curl performed at 80o for example also increases strength at other angles to a lesser extent. The same phenomenon is true for the knee and plantar flexors.

Essentially, training at only one joint angle does not increase strength throughout the full range of motion. In order to improve dynamic power, isometric exercises would have to be performed at multiple joint angles for the same muscle group. This becomes time consuming and enervating for an athlete who may already be spending considerable time on other training modalities.

If static strength training is used to increase strength throughout the entire range of motion, isometric exercises should be performed at every 10 to 30 degree increments. If this is too time consuming, it is better to perform exercises at an extended joint angle as this leads to greater cross-transference of strength at other angles.

2

Speed Training

Speed is the ability to reach a high velocity of movement in whatever mode of locomotion - running, cycling, skating swimming etc. Very often, agility is more relevant to successful sports performance than all-out speed. Agility is the ability to explosively brake, change direction and accelerate again.

Another element of fitness closely related to speed training is speed endurance. Many athletes must maintain a high velocity for longer than 6 seconds or produce repeated sprints with minimal rest periods in between. The combination of speed, agility and speed endurance an athlete requires is determined by his or her sport. But regardless of the event, there are several modes of training that are integral to developing a 'fast' athlete:

Strength and Power Training

Speed is chiefly determined by the capacity to apply a large amount of force in a short period of time. This is also known as power. Many athletic movements take place in 0.1 to 0.2 seconds but maximal force production takes 0.6 to 0.8 seconds. The athlete who can apply most force in the short period of available time is said to be the most powerful.

Strength training increases maximal force production. Assuming as a result, more force can be produced in the same period of time, strength training alone can increase power. However, it makes more sense to increase both maximal force production and the rate of force development. This can be achieved through power training. Both strength and power training are integral to improvement of speed.

Practising moving and accelerating faster helps to condition the neuromuscular system to improve the firing patterns of fast twitch muscle fibers. Two variations of basic speed training are assisted and resisted speed training. Assisted training (also called overspeed training helps to improve stride frequency. Resisted speed training helps to improve speed-strength and stride length.

Agility Training

Most team sports consist of very few movements that occur only in a straight line. Nor do those movements occur at a fixed pace or for a fixed length of time. Agility and quickness training improves an athlete's ability to change direction, brake suddenly and perform sport-specific skills with speed and dexterity.

How to Design a Speed Training Program

The complete speed training program aims to:

— Improve acceleration

— Increase maximal velocity

— Maintain velocity against the onset of fatigue

Closely related to speed training is agility and quickness training. This aims to:

— Decrease reactive ability and reaction time

— Improve deceleration

— Enhance the ability to change direction
— Improve co-ordination and dynamic balance

Speed and agility training are not the same and one does not necessarily improve the other. For example, straight-line sprinting has been shown to have little or no effect on agility tests that involve various changes of direction even though it improves 30meter sprint time. This has obvious implications for many athletes that rarely have to run in straight lines but are involved in regular, quick changes of direction. This chapter sets out the guidelines for increasing speed and agility. While some components of fitness (such as strength, power and basic speed) are relevant to most athletes, other elements of fitness covered here (such as speed-endurance and agility) are not applicable to all.

An obvious example is the 100meter sprinter compared to a soccer player. The sprinter's speed training program will focus predominantly on acceleration and maximal velocity in a straight line, whereas the soccer player rarely, if ever, reaches top speed. He or she will benefit from greater emphasis on agility training.

Strength and Power Training

There is a high correlation between an athlete's strength and explosive power and their sprint performance. This is usually measured with power tests such as jump squats, reactive jumps and short sprints and strength testing.

Conditioning can significantly increase performance in these tests so from deductive logic alone strength and power training can improve an athlete's speed. During the early pre-season phase of training, the emphasis is placed on developing maximal strength. The more force a muscle can produce, the more potential there is for greater power and speed. Of course the other element of the power equation is the speed of muscle contraction or the rate of force development.

A bodybuilder or weightlifter may be exceptionally strong but lack significant power if they are unable to apply that strength quickly. Similarly, individuals that can contract their muscles and move their limbs very rapidly are not necessarily the fastest athletes as they may not be able to generate significant force with each foot strike. Once a phase of maximal strength training has been completed it can be converted into explosive power through plyometric training for example.

Sprinting Technique

While other elements of the speed training program aim to condition the metabolic and neuromuscular systems, technique training results in a more efficient use of energy. Of course, it's not only elite sprint athletes that can benefit from examining and correcting their sprinting technique. Working on running biomechanics is low intensity and should not aim to fatigue the athlete. It should be completed before strenuous training and can even form the back-end of the warm up.

Basic Speed Training

While strength and power training alone can increase an athlete's speed, combining it with sprint training is more effective. Basic sprints help to improve reaction time, acceleration, top speed and deceleration. Keeping the exercise intervals short (i.e. <20 seconds) or the work to rest ratio relatively high (i.e. 1:5), prevents blood lactate from accumulating. Sprints can be repeated at near maximal velocity, which is necessary to induce the right neuromuscular adaptations.

A basic speed training program can be adapted by running uphill and downhill. Incline running helps to improve power during hip flexion and extension. Downhill running is effective at improving co-ordination and stride frequency.

Agility Training

Liner speed training aims to improve speed and acceleration and requires maximal effort and near maximal velocity. This is best achieved when running in a straight line. However, most team sports require rapid declaration and changes in direction. Agility training aims to convert basic speed into sport-specific speed.

As with basic sprint training, the work to rest ratio should allow adequate recovery between intervals and sets. Agility training relies on a high degree of co-ordination and movement quality, which becomes difficult in the presence of fatigue. Many of the coaching points for proper sprinting technique can be applied to agility training.

Sprint technique, basic speed training and agility training should all occur at the start of a training session when the athlete is fresh. A 20minute period is enough to combine basic sprints, technique practise and agility drills or they can be split up over several training days.

Speed Endurance Training

A 'fast' athlete can not only accelerate and move in multiple directions rapidly, they should also have the ability to repeat rapid movements with minimal loss of speed. In multi-sprint sports such as hockey and basketball, players are often required to repeat several high intensity runs, all-out sprints and sharp changes in direction without rest. This type of activity leads to rapid blood lactate accumulation severely hindering peak power and rate of force development.Training can help to curb lactate accumulation and increase the rate of clearance. For many athletes, the introduction of one or two speed endurance sessions during the latter stages of pre-season training is an important component of the overall speed training program.

A speed endurance session is created by reducing the work to rest ratio (i.e. 1:1) and increasing the work intervals (i.e. >30 seconds). Unlike basic speed and agility training, speed endurance conditioning is highly fatiguing and energy depleting. For this reason it may be more appropriate for skill and tactical work to occur beforehand in the training session.

Periodisation of a Speed Training Program

As with other components of conditioning, the speed training program varies over the course of the year. How much emphasis it is given at any point in the season obviously depends on the sport (i.e. 100meter sprinter versus basketball player). For team sports the following model is an example of how speed training changes over the course of a competitive year:

Early pre-season

The emphasis is on building a general conditioning base with maximal strength training and endurance training. Little or no sprint work is completed at this time. Sprinting technique can be addressed here if it is a particular concern for the athlete. Because it is non-fatiguing and low intensity it won't interfere with other forms of training during this phase.

Late pre-season

Strength is converted into explosive power with plyometric training or ballistics for example. Basic speed training and agility training is now incorporated into the overall program. It can take up to 8 weeks for before a conditioning response is seen, which may mean there is some overlap into the competitive season.

In-season

Speed and agility training is maintained. This can be achieved in 1-2 sessions per week at the start of a longer, mixed training session.

Transition /closed season

This phase is used for active recovery and regeneration. All speed training can be ceased and muscle balance issues addressed.

How to Improve Your Sprinting Technique

By breaking sprinting technique into its component parts you can focus on and improve specific phases of the action. Good sprinting technique has some of the following characteristics:

Start phase

i) Bodyweight evenly distributed over four contact points in the start position (i.e. hands and knees). Front knee angle is ~90°, rear knee angle ~100-130°.

i ii iii

ii) Explosive push off with both legs. Front leg extends remaining in contact with the ground while back leg swings forward. Extended front leg and trunk form a straight line.

iii) Arms swing opposite to legs, elbows flex to ~90° and fists swing towards forehead.

Accleration phase

iv) After first two strides, foot touches down in front of center of gravity.

v) Forward body lean begins to decrease until normal sprinting position is reached after about 22 yards (20 meters). Head is relaxed, eyes focused straight ahead.

iv v

Maximum speed phase

vi) Push-off angle from ground is ~50-55°. Trunk is almost erect with ~5° forward lean.

vii) (Midflight) Push-off leg folds tightly towards buttocks in a relaxed 'heeling' motion. Front leg thrusts forward and upward at maximum speed (~44mph in elite sprinters). When front thigh reaches maximum possible knee lift, lower leg swings forward in a relaxed movement.

viii) Foot meets ground with ankle slightly extended (plantar flexion) directly under center of gravity.

Bodyweight is balanced so that only the ball of the foot touches the ground.

ix) Shoulders remain steady, elbows flexed at ~90°, kept close to body throughout all phases. Hands swing forward and up above shoulder height, down and past hips. Arms and hands should have an aggressive hammering action. Head aligns naturally with trunk and shoulders and facial/neck muscles are relaxed by keeping the mouth slightly open.

Sprinting Technique Program

These sprinting technique drills can be performed in this order or alternatively focus on just 3-4 drills. There is no need to perform multiple sets and repetitions.

Raise Knees: 10 meters - jog - 10 meters - rest

Sprint 10 meters concentrating on raising knees as higher than normal. Jog for 10 meters and then sprint for 10 meters and rest.

Fast Knee Pick Ups: 10 meters - jog - 10 meters - rest

Jogging on the spot raise your knees to waist height while emphasising arm action. Move forward 10 meters with this action concentrating on the number of ground contacts rather than how fast you cover the distance. Try to get as many ground contacts as possible.

Flicks: 10 meters - jog - 10 meters - rest

While sprinting over 10 meters concentrate on flicking your heels up to touch your butt.

Leg Speed: 60 meters

This is a normal sprint over 60 meters except all of your focus should be on your legs. Try to gauge the optimum leg speed for you by taking different stride lengths to see which yields the best results.

Skipping: 40 meters

High Hops: 3 x 40 meters

Bound from one foot to the other. The action is similar to skipping except your are trying to gain as much height as possible and stay in the air for as long as possible. Remember to recover fully between attempts.

Elbow Drive: 40 meters

Sprint for 40 meters concentrating on driving your elbow in a straight line. Keep your elbows flexed at right angles while keeping your arms relaxed.

Sample Speed Training Drills

These sample speed training drills are designed to develop quick feet, power and acceleration. Use them as part of a more comprehensive speed program or as a session on their own. You can get more information on speed training by visiting the speed training section. Here some general guidelines are:

— A typical speed session might consist of 5 sets of 10 repetitions in total. You could do 1 set of each of the speed training drills below or choose 3 drills and do 1-2 sets of 10 sprints for each.

— Try to keep a work to rest ratio of 5:1. For example a 6 second sprint should be followed by approximately 30 seconds walking recovery.

— Speed training drills are best performed when you are fresh. Don't attempt these drills after a long endurance run or a heavy strength training session for example.

— It goes without saying that you should be fully warmed up before starting a speed training session. Do at least 10 mins light aerobic exercise followed by some dynamic stretches.

— Avoid static stretcing in the warm up. These are best left until the end of the session when increasing/ maintaining flexibility is important.

Speed Training Drills

Drill 1 - bounding

This is a plyometrics exercise. Along with a strength training program, plyometrics will help to improve your sprinting power.

1. Jog into the start of the drill for forward momentum.
2. After a few feet, forcefully push off with the left foot and bring the leg forward. At same time drive your right arm forward.
3. Repeat with other leg and arm.
4. This exercise is an exaggerated running motion focusing on foot push-off and air time.

Drill 2 - Alternating strides

Speed training drills like these help to develop foot speed and co-ordination.

1. Set up a series of cones in a straight line. The first 10 cones should be about 1 meter/yard apart. The next 10 should be 2 meters/yards apart.
2. From standing start sprint the total length of the cones taking one step between each marker.
3. The cones close together will encourage faster, shorter strides. You can gradually decrease the distance between cones as you progress. Walk slowly back to the start to recover.

Drill 3 - Alternating Starts

The basis of these speed training drills is a 10-20 meter/ yard sprint. You should focus on accelerating as quickly as possible by powering away with your arms and legs. If your sport involves reacting quickly from different starting positions (as most sports do) try to vary the starting position. Examples include doing a press up then sprinting, sitting on your hands, lying face down, doing 5 squat jumps before sprinting etc.

Drill 4 - Accelerating Sprints

This drill requires you to mark out distance of about 100 yards/meters where you can sprint in a straight line. You also need to mark a halfway point either with some landmark or a mark on the ground. Starting at one end, gradually accelerate to reach full speed at the halfway point and continue to sprint to the end. Slow down gradually to a jog, turn and walk/jog back to the start. Speed training drills like these help to develop speed and power endurance. Remember though the emphasis should be on the quality of the sprint so allow plenty of time to recover as you walk between sprints.

Drill 5 - Weave In/Weave Out

This is an excellent drill for developing lateral (sideways) agility.

1. Place 4 cones in a straight line about 3 yards/meters apart.
2. In between each pair of cones place another cone about 3 yards/meters to the left.
3. Sprint from one cone to the next touching each one with your hand.
4. Try to take quick side steps, rather than turning to face the marker and running forward.

Sample Speed & Agility Drills

These speed and agility drills are designed to improve your speed off the mark and acceleration. For multi-sprint sports such as basketball, soccer and tennis absolute speed is not the most important factor. Speed off the mark, acceleration and agility are...

How often does a basketball player have to sprint over long distances (50 to 100meters) in a straight line? The point to remember is that you don't have to be blessed with the genetic makeup of a Carl Lewis to be quick in many sports. With a little training and practise you can run 5 yards while your opponent is still thinking about it. If you're a sprint athlete then absolute speed is a major determining factor of your success. Speed off the mark and acceleration are still key elements however.

General Guidelines for Speed And Agility Drills

Quality is the key for successful performance of these speed and agility drills. Keep the individual sprints short and rest completely between sets. Use these 6 pointers to optimise the training response:

1. Warm up thoroughly. Speed and agility drills may not leave you out of breath but they do put considerable strain on your musculature.
2. Speed and agility drills should be performed either on separate days to other training or at the start of a training session after the warm up.
3. You will gain most benefit from these speed and agility drills if you have previously developed a solid strength and power base.
4. A typical session may consist of approximately 5 sets of 10 repetitions (each sprint being 1 repetition). Work to rest ratio should be 1:5 i.e. a 5 second sprint should be followed by a 25 second recovery period.
5. The number of sessions per week varies greatly. For most team sports speed and agility drills should be introduced late on in the pre-season phase. Two sessions a week is usually adequate. During the competitive season, one session per week may be enough. Sprint athletes may need as many as 3-5 sessions per week.

6. The speed and agility drills below are suitable for many sports. To make them more specific adapt them slightly to mirror the movement patterns in your game.

Speed and Agility Drills

1. Basic sprints

Set 2 cones out 10-20 meters apart. Sprint from one cone to the next and slowly jog back to the start. Vary the start of the sprint to make the drill more sport specific. For example. Face backwards, lie down, jump up, pretend to receive a pass, jump to head a ball etc.

2. Rolling start

Exactly the same as above except you jog for 10 meters before sprinting. This drill is specifically designed to enhance acceleration rather than speed off the mark. Try running backwards or side stepping as well.

3. Up hill sprints

In competition the first few strides are crucial. Running up a slight hill (about 30 degrees) helps to develop power and acceleration. Keep the distances short (10-15 meters) and allow extra rest between sets and reps. An alternative to uphill running is a resistance parachute. Resistance chutes are one of the most popular and effective training aids for sprinters. If it's adjustable it can be used to develop power for sprint trainers or even long distance runners.

4. Down hill sprints (over speed training)

Down hill speed and agility drills help to develop leg speed and co-ordination. This is sometimes referred to as over-speed training. Keep the distance short (10-15 meters) and make sure the hill is only slight. An alternative method of over-speed training is to use elastic cords. An Over-Speed Trainer consists of a pulley system to provide a smooth build up of speed. It enables the sprinter to move at a rate greater than 100% of their usual top speed. It can also be used to provide resistance much like uphill sprints.

5. Hollow sprints

Set 5 cones out in 30 meters intervals. Sprint 30 meters, jog 30 meters, sprint 30 meters and jog 30 meters to the final cone. Walk back to the start and repeat.

6. Cruise and sprint

Mark out a distance of 100 meters. From the start gradually accelerate to reach full speed at about 60 meters. Sprint all out for the final 40 meters. Reduce the number of repetitions for this exercise as it takes longer to complete.

7. Ladder drills

A ladder is a simple training device that helps to improve co-ordination and leg speed. It can be used for a number of speed and agility drills and is particularly useful for sports such as tennis and basketball that requires fast and co-ordinated footwork.

8. The snake

Set up a series of 6-8 cones in a straight line about 1 meter apart. Weave through the cones, turn and weave through back to the start.

9. Follow the Leader

A training partner and large area is required for this drill. Have your training partner jog, run and sprint randomly over a large area. You must try to shadow her as closely as possible. This is an excellent drill that helps to develop reaction time, acceleration and speed endurance.

Speed Endurance Training

The speed endurance drills will help you to maintain a higher work rate for longer. They are excellent for improving performance in sports such as football, soccer, hockey and basketball. Any athlete that is required to repeat high intensity sprints in quick succession can benefit from this type of training.

The accumulation of blood lactate disturbs the excitation-contraction coupling and cross-bridge formation. In other words, the muscle's mechanical properties are disturbed. The result? A decrease in force production, peak force and velocity. Training can improve the clearance rate of lactate and reduce early lactate formation.

Both submaximal aerobic exercise and interval training can improve the body's ability to buffer and tolerate lactate. However, only intense interval training can increase various important components of anaerobic power and capacity. Submaximal aerobic exercise does not and may even decrease anaerobic enzyme activity. Speed endurance training is similar to speed or sprint training, however there are two important distinctions:

1. Repetitions should last from 30 seconds up to 2-3 minutes as opposed to 5-10 seconds for speed drills.
2. Rest intervals between repetitions is reduced to prevent complete recovery.

Speed Endurance Drills

Speed endurance training should form the later part of pre-season training and in-season training. It is important to develop a solid fitness base beforehand, which includes strength and endurance conditioning. No more than two speed endurance sessions are required. This may be reduced to once a week during the competitive season. Because speed endurance training can be so demanding, keep session duration to 20-30 minutes maximum. Rest intervals should consist of active recovery exercises such as walking or jogging slowly on the spot.

High intensity shuttle run

— Pace out 30 meters on grass or a running track. Place a cone at the start and at 5 meter intervals (7 cones in total).

— Sprint from the starting cone to 5 meter cone and back. Turn and sprint to 10 meter cone and back to start. Sprint to 15meter cone and back to start and so on until you sprint the full 30 meters and back.

— Rest for 90 seconds and repeat. Complete a total of 6 sets keeping rest periods to 90 seconds.

Pyramids

— Pace out 50 meters placing a cone at the start and then at 10 meter intervals (6 cones in total).

— Starting at the first cone sprint all out for 10 meters and walk the remaining 40 meters.

— Turn and sprint 20 meters and walk for 30 meters.

— Turn and sprint 30 meters and walk for 20 meters.

— Turn and sprint 40 meters and walk for 10 meters.

— Turn and sprint 50 meters and then turn and sprint 50 meters again back to the start.

— This is classed as one set. Rest for 90 seconds and repeat for a total of 4 sets. Rest for a full 3 minutes and repeat.

Cruise and sprint

— Mark out a distance of 100 meters. From the start gradually accelerate to reach full speed at about 60 meters. Sprint all out for the final 40 meters.

— Slow down gradually, turn and repeat.

— Continue for 2 minutes and then rest for 2 minutes. This is one set. Repeat for a total of 6 sets.

Hollow sprint

— Set 5 cones out in 30 meters intervals. Sprint 30 meters, jog 30 meters, sprint 30 meters and jog 30 meters to the final cone.

— Turn around and repeat always alternating jogging and sprinting. Work for 2 minutes and then rest for 2 minutes.

— This is one set. Try to complete a total of 6 sets.

Cross drill

— Using 4 cones mark a box 30 meters by 30 meters. Place another cone in the center of the box.

— Starting at the center cone sprint to each corner and back in a clockwise direction. Once you have completed a circuit rest for 60 seconds.

— Perform a total of 6 circuits to complete one set. A session could contain up to 4 sets with a 3 minute rest interval between sets.

Speed Training For Football

Football is not just about strength.In fact speed training for football might be just as important as traditional weight lifting. The highest ranked players are more likely to outperform their peers in tests like the 10 yard and 40 yards sprints than they are in the squat or bench press.

You could say that speed separates the outstanding from the very good. But you certainly don't have to be the fastest to perform at your best. Which do you think is more important? Acceleration or top speed?

Consider this for a moment. The average distance a football player covers in most plays is 15-20 yards (maybe less for a lineman and more for a receiver). Unlike an Olympic sprinter, football players will rarely, if ever, reach their top speed. On the whole, the quickest player over 15-20 yards will be the one who can accelerate the most rapidly.

Straight away then, that should tell you something about speed training for football - running lots of 100m sprints is not an effective method of training. Instead, spend your time on drills that increase acceleration and speed off the mark.

How to Increase Your Speed & Acceleration

It's true - genetics do play a part in how fast you can run. But don't let that discourage you. Everyone can get faster. And anyone can improve their speed off the mark. And just a small improvement with training relates to a significant improvement on the field. With that said, what does it take to increase your sprinting speed?

1. Increase your strength

— The more powerful your leg muscles are the more force they can apply to each ground contact.

— Power is a product of both strength and speed of contraction. If you make improvements in either of these components you will become a faster athlete.

— Improve both and you double the effects - and this it what speed training for football is essentially all about.

— Assuming strength training already contributes a significant amount to your schedule, lets look at the other side of the equation.

2. Improve your speed of contractions

— Any increase in strength will only translate into gains in speed IF you can still contract your muscles as quickly - ideally even quicker.

— Sprint training over short distances will help you do that. So will some light plyometrics exercises.

— The science behind plyometrics or jump training can get a little complex but the actual training is straightforward.

— Be careful with plyometric training.

— It's easy to overtrain without knowing it. Too many of these exercises (particularly the intense types) can cause stress injuries.

3. Improve your running mechanics

— Most football players, in fact most sports men and women have never been taught correct sprinting form.

— All other things being equal, the more efficiently you can run, the faster you can run.

— There are basically two phases to sprinting - the acceleration phase and top speed phase. Remember acceleration is probably more important in speed training for football than top speed. Here are some pointers for good acceleration form...

  — Drive off the balls of your feet never the toes or heels.

  — The whole body should be leaning forward, not just from the waist.

— Strides are short and powerful, pushing off the ground.

— Pump the arms vigorously throwing the elbow back hard rather than forward

— Keep the head still and square to the shoulders.

After the first 10-15 yards, running mechanics change noticeably as you gain speed.

— Foot strikes should still be from the balls of the feet.

— There is still a slight forward lean from the ground but much less.

— Strides are longer and more relaxed. Don't try to push away from the ground.

— Arm action is still exaggerated but more relaxed.

— Head remains still.

As part of a season long plan, speed training for football features heavily in late pre-season preparation and gradually increases over the whole of pre-season. It should also follow a period of base strength training for maximum results.

Soccer Speed Training

At any level, speed separates the outstanding players from the average. So, soccer speed training sessions should play a major role in your training. Speed in soccer can be quite complex. It certainly entails more than just running fast. When you talk about speed in your game, here are some of the attributes that will make you a better player...

— Quick speed off the mark

— Quick acceleration over 10-15 yards

— Good speed endurance

— Speed in possession of the ball

— Quickness of feet or agility
— The ability to quickly change direction
— The ability to execute skills quickly
— Last but not least... speed of thought

You can see from the above that good 100m sprinters don't necessarily have the attributes to be quick soccer players. And by the same token.

Players who are not typically fast runners can excel in soccer if they have sharp feet and quick speed of thought.

Absolute speed or your ability to run fast is determined by a number of factors - the obvious one being genetics.

But if you've been blessed with less than favourable sprinting genes don't worry too much.

A good soccer speed training program will improve the efficiency of your muscle fibres and that will make you faster.

So, one goal of your soccer speed training schedule should be to increase your sprinting power - particularly your acceleration and speed off the mark. Soccer players rarely sprint more than 50 yards in a straight line.

A second, and equally important, goal is to increase your speed endurance.

Speed endurance training significantly improves your recovery after a bout of repetitive sprints. Your body's ability to remove lactic acid increases which can make such a difference to your game.

Thirdly, a soccer speed training program should improve agility, foot speed and reaction time. Exercises to improve agility don't tend to be physically taxing. The emphasis is on short, sharp movements of a high quality.

Finally, incorporating a ball into some of the speed and agility drills is important to make all those gains in speed transferable to the field of play.

How to Improve Your Speed & Sprinting Power

Before we move on to agility and fast feet, let's look at how training can significantly improve absolute speed and acceleration. There are 4 important elements that will make you a faster athlete...

1. Strength and power training

Power relates directly to absolute speed. 100m sprinters are very powerful. So are footballers. Weight lifters are very strong - but not necessarily as powerful.

Power is a combination of both strength and speed of contraction. Increase either one and you increase power. Ideally, you want to increase both.

Weight training increases strength and plyometric training "converts" that strength into speed and power.

2. Sprint training

To improve speed off the mark, running mechanics and acceleration training should feature in your soccer speed training routine. It doesn't have to be much - just one short session a week before practice is enough during the in-season.

Drills should be completed over short distances with plenty of rest between sprints. The idea is not to tire yourself. Concentrate on form and speed of leg movement over the first few yards.

Over the course of a season, start sprint drills in mid to late pre-season and continue right through the in-season. Because they aren't fatiguing you can perform they the day before a game. A lot of pros teams feel that they help to increase mental sharpness in preparation for an upcoming game. As a side note, sprint drills should be performed at the start of a training session when you are fresh.

3. Speed endurance training

Be prepared - this type of training can be a killer. A few athletes I know have nicknames for some of these drills. None of them are repeatable here!

But from a personal perspective, the rewards are worth the temporary "discomfort" you feel after (and during) a short session.

As you can probably gather these drills are intense. They are designed to generate large amounts of lactic acid quickly. That way your body adapts by increasing its removal and dramatically speeding up your recovery. What does this have to do with speed?

Soccer is a multi-sprint sport and there are many occasions over 90 minutes when you are forced to make repeated sprints in quick succession. Your ability to maintain high percentage of your speed and power relies, in part, on your body's ability to remove lactic acid.

There's nothing worse than receiving the ball after several sprints chasing opponents - as they triangles around you! Try doing a Cruyff turn then!

From personal experience, as taxing as these speed endurance drills are they make a game feel easy. It's a real confidence booster and well worth the effort.

During mid to late pre-season you can perform 2 speed endurance sessions a week (separated by 24-48 hours).

4. Flexibility training

It's always an uphill struggle trying to get athletes to

stretch for the purpose of increasing their range of motion. They'll do it to warm-up but there are so many benefits to moderately increasing range of motion.

One of them is increasing power and speed of motion. A muscle can only contract as fast as its opposing muscle can relax. Flexibility training can release tightness and promote this speed of relaxation.

Increasing range of motion also helps to lengthen leg stride and is important for quick and agile changes in direction.

Try to do some stretching exercises three times a week - following a training session when muscles are warm.

How to Improve Your Quickness & Agility

Agility defines your ability to accelerate, decelerate and change direction quickly, whilst maintaining speed, body control and poise. Often times you have to do this while in possession of the ball.

Whereas strength, power and all-out sprint training are designed to improve your maximum speed, agility and quickness drills help to increase the speed of finer movements. They improve co-ordination, balance and foot speed.

You can easily combine agility exercises and sprint training exercises into one session - or even a part of one session (usually at the beginning).

If you've ever seen an athlete use an agility ladder they are training to improve foot speed. But you don't need anything other than a set of marker cones and a little creativity to design effective drills.

You should also try to use a ball in some of the drills, although it's not the time to try elaborate skills. Typically, if you're using a ball, you should touch it the minimum of times and focus on the movement between touches.

To wrap up, soccer speed training incorporates several components of fitness and a number of different types of training modalities.

Thinking that you've got to make time for sprint training, speed endurance training, agility drills AND then strength training and plyometrics can be a bit disheartening. Remember though...

Most of these drills can be combined into one practise. No need to have a separate session for agility drills and sprint training.

Not all types of training can or should be performed at the same point in the season. A plyometrics session substitutes a weights session for example.

A Complete Soccer Speed Training System

Speed and agility training in covered in-depth, as is every element of fitness important in the game.

— Strength and strength endurance training
— Speed and agility training
— Aerobic and anaerobic endurance training
— Flexibility, warming up and cooling down
— Testing soccer-specific fitness
— Nutrition for soccer
— Off-season, pre-season and in-season program design

3

Power Training

Power training enables an athlete to apply the greatest amount of their maximal strength in the shortest period of time. This is crucial for many sports men and women who will rarely be required nor have the time to produce maximal forces.

Most athletic activities involve far faster movements and far higher power outputs than are found in maximal strength exercises. An athlete can be exceptionally strong but lack significant explosive power if they are unable to apply their strength rapidly.

This outlines the various methods of power training, their parameters and how they can be used to convert maximal strength into sport-specific power. But before examining how power training should fit into the overall strength program, it's important to have a basic understanding of the relationship between the force of movement and the velocity of movement.

Force-Velocity Relationship

Power is intimately related to force and time, which can be expressed in the simple formula:

$$\text{Power} = \frac{\text{Force x Distance}}{\text{Time}}$$

Traditional strength training typically alters the top half of this equation - increasing the ability to apply a maximum amount of force. But for power to be maximised the time component must also be altered. This is the aim of power training - to reduce the amount of time it takes to apply a set amount of force.

Maximum force production occurs when the speed of movement is very low (i.e. performing a one repetition maximum lift) or zero such as performing a static or isometric exercise. Conversely, as the speed of movement increases, force decreases and at very high speeds force production is very low. Between these two extremes is an optimal point for power development. In fact, maximal power occurs at intermediate velocities when lifting moderate loads. Peak power output is typically seen when loads of 30% one repetition maximum (1-RM) are used.

This relationship between force and velocity and its affect on power explains why an athlete can be exceptionally strong but lack significant power if they are unable to apply much of their strength over a short period of time.

Assuming an athlete has maximised his or her ability to apply force (through maximal strength training), it would be beneficial if they could train to increase the rate of force production. Increasing the rate at which strength can be generated positively alters the time aspect of the power equation above. The goal of power training is to increase the rate of force production and there are several methods that have been devised to do this.

Types of Power Training

Below are four methods of power training. A prerequisite to starting one of these routines is the development of a solid base of functional strength. Power training, particularly plyometrics and ballistics, becomes less effective and the risk of injury is increased if a phase of anatomical adaptation has not already been completed.

Heavy strength training

Strength training alone can increase explosive power by positively affecting the top half of the power equation or the peak force production. Most athletic movements also start from a stationary position and it is this early phase of moving a resistance (be it a medicine ball or bodyweight) that requires the most effort. Therefore the greater an athlete's strength is, the more explosive this initial phase of motion will be. However, once this initial inertia has been overcome less force and more speed is required to continue the movement and heavy strength training becomes less suitable.

Additionally, lifting weights of 70-100% 1-RM has also been shown to reduce the rate of force production which is counter-productive to power development. This may explain why in strength trained individuals heavy resistance training is less effective at increasing vertical jump performance compared to ballistics or plyometrics for example. For an athlete who already has a solid base of strength training (+6 months) gains in power are minimal with further weight training. Of course, untrained individuals can significantly improve their power with weight training and this is a safer and more favorable mode of training than some of the advanced techniques that follow.

Explosive strength training

Once a plateau in strength has been reached, more sport-specific types of power training are required. One of these training methods is a variation of traditional resistance training. As mentioned earlier, maximal power production occurs when moderate loads of about 30% 1-RM are used. Completing traditional weight lifting exercises as fast as possible with relatively light loads produces in theory, the greatest power output. Unfortunately there is a problem with this approach. Lifting a bar rapidly loaded with 30% 1-RM is difficult to execute, particularly in the final phase of the movement. The athlete must decelerate and stop the bar in order to keep it under control. This deceleration activates the antagonist muscles negatively affecting power output and hinders the required adaptations.

Ballistics and plyometrics avoid this problem, as there is no deceleration. The athlete is free to jump as high as possible or throw an object as far as possible without restricting the movement.

If free weights exercises are used for power training, loads of 75-85% are recommended for sets of 3-5 repetitions. For single power efforts such as the throwing events in athletics, a higher load (80-90% 1-RM) can be used for a smaller number of repetitions. A multiple power effort sport includes sprinting,team sports or any event that requires repeated efforts.

Sets are not performed to exhaustion as the quality and speed of each lift is the most important factor. Rest intervals are also kept high for the same reason.

Ballistics

During a ballistic action, the force far outweighs the resistance so movement is of a high velocity. The resistance is accelerated and projected. Examples include a medicine ball throw and a jump squat. The aim is to reach peak acceleration at the moment of release projecting the object or body as far as possible. While there is no definitive guidelines for the resistance used with ballistics, Fleck and Kraemer suggest a load of 30-35% 1-RM should be used for exercises that include free weights such as jump squats. For many ballistic exercises the weight of the objects themselves dictate the load i.e. medicine balls ranging from 2-6kg (4.4-13lbs) and kettlebells ranging from 10-32kg (22-70lbs). Parameters for ballistic power training are summarised in the table below:

Ballsitic Training Guidelines

Load (medicine balls)	Variable
Load	30% 1-RM
No. exercises	2-3
No. reps per set (medicine ball)	10-20
No. reps per set (30% 1-RM)	1-3
No. sets per session	3-5
Rest interval	2-3 minutes
Speed of execution	Explosive
Frequency	2-3 x per week

Repetitions can be reasonably high as the nature of some exercises means there can be up to 20 seconds between efforts - for example when a medicine ball has to be retrieved. A set should stop however, the moment the speed and quality of movement can no longer be maintained. For exercises such as jump squats that use

30% 1-RM loads, Fleck and Kraemer recommend up to 5 sets of 3 repetitions with 3 minutes rest between sets.

Ballistics can place considerable eccentric forces on joints, ligaments and tendons when landing from a jump squat for example. Athletes should always progress gradually from unloaded to loaded exercises and must not be fatigued before starting a ballistic power training session.

Plyometrics

Plyometric drills involve a quick, powerful movement using a pre-stretch or counter-movement that involves the stretch shortening cycle. Classical plyometric exercises include various types of jump training and upper body drills using medicine balls. Plyometrics is a suitable form of power training for many team and individual sports. While many might see it simply as jumping up and down, there are important guidelines and program design protocols that need to be followed if plyometrics is to be as safe and effective as possible.

The type of power training employed must be the most specific to the sport or event. Olympic lifts, such as power cleans, may be suitable for sports such as football and rugby. Some plyometric exercises are suitable for soccer and hockey. Ballistic exercises with medicine balls fit well with basketball and volleyball.

But many sports would benefit from a combination of power training methods. Take basketball for example - explosive strength training such as power cleans, plyometric exercises such as depth jumps and ballistics such as jump squats and overhead medicine ball throws would all be suitable choices.

Interestingly, a study measuring the effects of three types of power training found that all of them increased vertical jump performance. However, while traditional weight training lead to a 5% increase and plyometrics a 10% increase, the most effective was ballistic jump squats, which lead to an 18% improvement in jump height. This confirmed the findings of a similar earlier study. Does this mean ballistics is superior to other forms of power training? Not necessarily. In this case it may be that jump squats was the most specific to the performance outcome.

MUSCULAR ENDURANCE TRAINING

The combination of strength and endurance results in muscular endurance - the ability to perform many repetitions against a given resistance for a prolonged period of time. It is a crucial element of fitness for athletes such as distance runners, swimmers, cyclists and rowers. It's also important for success in many team sports like soccer, field hockey and Australian rules football.

Traditionally, muscular endurance programs have used moderate loads lifted for 12-25 repetitions. However, this is completely inadequate for many sports such as boxing, canoeing, distance running, cycling, swimming, rowing, x-country skiing, triathlon and many others. Any form of training must mirror the specific demands of the sport. In resistance training, this means that the load used should match the resistance that must be overcome while competing. The number of repetitions or the duration of exercise bouts in a session should approach that during the event.

Recall that muscular endurance training makes up only one part of the annual strength program - even for endurance athletes. It should follow a phase of maximal strength training. This makes sense because the greater an athlete's maximal strength, the greater their potential for strength endurance - i.e. the more force they will be able to apply over a prolonged period. Heavy strength training has also been shown to improve exercise economy in endurance athletes.

The Different Types of Muscular Endurance

Different sports require different levels of muscular endurance. While each program will vary according to the athlete's needs, muscular endurance can be split into 3 groups:

Power endurance

Athletes like baseball pitchers, sprinters, 50-m freestyle swimmers, martial artists, wrestlers, fencers, tennis players and so on must produce powerful movements and repeat them several times with little or no rest. In order to maintain the same amount of power with each effort, a certain level of power endurance is required.

Power endurance is typically characterised by intense, repeated efforts for a relatively short period of time (less than 30 seconds). A tennis player for example, has to produce several powerful shots in quick succession during a rally that may only last 10 seconds. A 100-m sprinter may take 48-54 powerful strides over a 10-12 second race and their success depends, in part, on maintaining a high power output in the last 20 meters.

Once maximal strength has been developed (earlier on in the annual strength program) it can be converted into explosive power through various methods of power training. Now power endurance training can be used to train the fast twitch fibres to resist fatgiue allowing explosive power to be maintained for longer.

Power endurance training uses moderate loads of 50-70% 1RM lifted for 15 to 30 repetitions. Because this can lead to a significant build up of lactic acid, rest periods between sets are long (5-7 minutes) and a minimum number of sport-specific exercises are used (about 3-4).

Exercises are also completed in a circuit training format i.e. one set of one exercise is completed, then one set of the next exercise and so on. Alternating exercises allows maximum recovery and sufficient time for lactic acid to disperse.

This is a critical rule to follow. If rest intervals are too short and sets are completed while the athlete is fatigued the result will be hypertrophy (increase muscle mass) rather than power endurance. Sets should not be completed to failure but should end when repetitions are no longer powerful and rhythmic.

Muscular endurance - short term

When sports and events consist predominantly of bouts of exercise lasting between 30 seconds and 2 minutes, "short-term" muscular endurance training is advantageous. These could be continuous events such as the 800-m or multi-sprint sports such as soccer.

Muscular endurance training helps athletes to cope with fatigue and tolerate high levels of lactic acid. It uses relatively light loads of 40-60% 1RM and they can be lifted for a set period of time or a target number of repetitions. Again, a circuit training set up is suitable for this type of resistance training.

Muscular endurance - long term

"Long term" muscular endurance is suitable for continuous, steady-state events such as the marathon, triathlon and rowing that last beyond 2 minutes. Light loads are used so that exercises can be sustained for a prolonged period. Rest periods are kept to a minimum and ideally the athlete should progress so that the only rest between exercises is the time it takes to move between equipment.

Concurrent Strength Training & Endurance Training: How Does One Affect the Other?

Designing an ideal strength training program for sport in itself can be a complex process. Yet resistance training is only one component of an athlete's overall training regime, which can also include endurance training, speed training, flexibility training and skill / tactical work.

Perhaps the most important element in a total conditioning program is adequate rest and recovery, without which the body cannot adapt properly to the imposed demands.

How does strength training interact with other components of fitness? Does endurance training have a negative effect on strength and power? And does strength and power training negatively effect aerobic power or flexibility?

This examines the integration of a sport-specific strength training plan into the total conditioning program and how any negative impact of concurrent training can be reduced. The body adapts specifically to the demands imposed upon it. So what happens when two different modes of training that place different stresses on the body are performed concurrently?

A number of studies have examined the compatibility of simultaneous strength and endurance training. In 1980, Hickson found that strength development maybe negatively effected by endurance training. Hunter and co-workers found that over a 12-week period a program of barbell squats only increased leg strength by 39%. This compared favourably to a program of squats and endurance training, which increased strength by just 24%.

Similar detriments to strength have been supported by other researchers. In contrast however, studies have also found that endurance training has no detrimental effect on strength development. Interestingly, although some of these studies found a negative effect on strength and some didn't, all agreed that concurrent strength and endurance training has no negative effect on endurance.

Strength at high velocities may be more vulnerable to endurance training than strength at slow speeds. This has obvious implications for power and speed performance which may be susceptible if a significant amount of endurance training is undertaken. Kraemer and fleck suggest that strength and endurance training programs with a moderate amount of volume seem to be compatible with no deleterious effects on either strength or endurance. As the volume increases to that adopted by elite athletes, detriments in strength are more likely to occur. It may be the overtraining phenomenon that is to blame rather than the incompatibility of concurrent strength and endurance training.

Concurrent Strength & Endurance Training: Effect on Endurance

Beginning in the 1970's many runners avoided resistance training for fear that it resulted in a decrease in endurance performance. This was based on studies that found a reduction in mitochondrial density following a resistance training program.

Subsequent research has found that strength training does not reduce endurance performance and mitochondrial density can actually increase as a result of a resistance training program.

There is evidence to suggest that strength training is beneficial to endurance performance in non-athletes. For example, time to exhaustion in a cycle ergometer test and lactate threshold can be increased without any change in VO2max. Strength training may also improve endurance performance in trained athletes. In one study on elite cyclists, 30-second sprint performance decreased with heavy endurance training. By adding resistance training to the program, sprint performance was maintained without any negative effects on endurance.

Additionally, by substituting 32% of total endurance training in elite distance runners for strength training, 5km performance has been improved significantly. Substantial endurance training may be detrimental to strength and power athletes. In endurance sports, strength training applied correctly appears to have an ergogenic effect without altering VO2max.

Strength Training & Flexibility

The flexibility training section of the site discuses the effect of stretching as part of the warm up. Recent research has found that pnf stretching can hinder vertical jump performance. Static stretching may also be detrimental to subsequent power performance.

These post-stretch decreases in force production may be related to the inactivation of the muscles affected - more so than a change in elasticity often thought to be the cause. Evidence that static or pnf stretching immediately prior to power and speed events harms performance is by no means conclusive and studies have also shown it to have no negative effects. The general consensus seems to favor dynamic stretching as part of the warm up and static stretching following exercise or a training session. While the debate continues, how do the long-term adaptations associated with strength training affect flexibility?

One study measuring the effects of 11 weeks of resistance training on range of movement found that ankle dorsiflexion and shoulder rotation both increased without any flexibility training. Research in the elderly has found that resistance training alone can in increase performance in the sit and reach test by 13%.

While these increases in range of motion can be quite marked in sedentary individuals, the effect of strength conditioning on flexibility in trained individuals is less pronounced. For example, weightlifters posses average to above average flexibility in most joints. This would suggest that long-term physiological changes that occur through lifting weights neither significantly increase nor reduce range of motion.

For athletes, perhaps more important than the extent of flexibility is the ability to control movements within a given range of motion. For example, a martial artist may be able to kick to head height but lack any significant power or control at that joint angle. Strength training and concurrent flexibility training can help to control movements within an athlete's current range of movement.

Dumbell Exercises for Every Major Muscle Group

Dumbell exercises are popular with recreational gym users right through to elite athletes. They can be used exclusively to form a wide variety of strength training programs, or they can be used to compliment a program that uses resistance machines, barbells or resistance bands for example.

Dumbells are often favored over weights machines and when performed correctly they are equally as safe. Dumbell exercises incorporate stabilising muscles helping to develop a balanced posture and perhaps reducing the risk of over-use injuries. They also allow you to work through a potentially greater range of movement than resistance machines.

General guidelines for dumbell exercises

Dumbell exercises are extremely safe when performed correctly. The following guidelines are not only for your safety, they are important to maintain the quality of the workout helping you achieve the results you set out to.

1. *Complete a warm up:* Perform 5-10 minutes of light aerobic exercise followed by stretching exercises to all major muscle groups.
2. *Start with a light weight:* Correct form is essential in order to avoid injury and get the most from these dumbbell exercises. Start with a low weight and only increase the resistance is proper technique can be maintained.
3. *Use a spotter:* Ideally you should have someone 'spot' each of the dumbell exercises you perform. Spotting involves carefully watching the lifts and being ready to intervene should the lifter require help. This is particularly important when sets are completed to exhaustion or failure.
4. *Avoid dropping dumbells:* It may be tempting to drop or throw the dumbells to the floor once an exercise has been completed rather than lowering under control. However, whilst you are holding the weights your muscles are under considerable tension and suddenly dropping them will release this tension rapidly (like firing an elastic band) increasing the risk of muscle tears. Some dumbell exercises permit relatively heavy weights to be used that are awkward to lower safely. In this a case spotter should assist the lifter.
5. *Designing a program:* The dumbell exercises you select, the amount of weight you use and the number of sets and repetitions you complete depends on your training outcome. Dumbell exercises can be used to develop maximal strength, strength endurance, explosive power or increased muscle mass. For sample weight training programs that focus on different elements of strength see the strength training section

Chest dumbell exercises

Flat dumbell press

Works the pectorals, triceps and the anterior deltoid (front of shoulder).

1. Lying flat on a bench, hold the weights directly above your chest, arms extended and palms facing towards your feet.
2. Lower the weights to your chest under control.
3. Press the dumbells back up to the starting position and repeat.
4. Avoid locking your elbows. This keeps the tension in your pectoral muscles and prevents joint damage.

Incline dumbell press

A variation of the flat press, this exercise works the upper pectorals, triceps and the anterior deltoid.

1. Adjust the bench to an incline of 30 to 45 degrees.
2. Perform a dumbell press.

Flat Flies

1. Lying flat on a bench, hold the weights directly above your chest. Palms facing towards each other.
2. Bend your elbows slightly and maintain this flexion for the rest of the exercise.
3. Open your arms in an arc lowering the weights. Your elbows should remain 'locked' in a slightly bent position. Imagine opening your arms to give someone a hug and you won't go far wrong!
4. When your upper arms are parallel to the floor, use the same movement to return the weights to the starting position and repeat.

Incline flies

1. Adjust the bench to an incline of 30 to 45 degrees.
2. Perform the exercise

Shoulder Dumbell Exercises

Seated shoulder press

Works all 3 heads of the deltoid (shoulder) muscle.

1. Sit upright on the end of the bench with the dumbells extended directly above your head. Make sure your back is not rounded. Adjust the bench so it forms an upright chair to support your back if necessary.
2. Lower the weights slowly and under control to your shoulders.
3. When your arms are bent to 90 degrees, press the dumbells back up without locking your elbows and repeat.

Lateral raises

Most dumbell exercises are superior to the machine equivelent. This one is no exception. Out of all the dumbell exercises described this is also the one that is invariably performed badly. If you keep good form you cannot lift a heavy weight.

1. Stand upright, knees slightly bent and shoulder width apart, holding the dumbells at your sides.
2. Bend you elbows slightly and raise the dumbells out to the side. Keep you elbows slightly bent as you do this.
3. When your arms are parallel to the floor, slowly lower the weights back down and repeat.

4. If you catch yourself arching your back, dipping your knees or bringing your shoulders back use a lighter weight.

Reverse flies

Works the posterior (rear) deltoid. The exercise is performed as its name suggests. It's simply a chest fly in reverse.

1. Sit on the edge of a bench, feet flat on the floor and knees bent at right angles. Bend right over so your chest is almost resting on your thighs.
2. Hold 2 dumbells next to your feet and bend your arms slightly. Open your arms out in an arc keeping your elbows bent.
3. When your arms are parallel to the floor slowly lower the weights back to the ground with the same motion.
4. You can and should only use a light weight for this exercise. If you find it places too much strain on your lower back try this variation...

Adjust the bench as though you are about to perform an incline dumbell press. Lie face down and let your arms hang down so your knuckles brush the floor. From here perform the movement described above.

Front raises

Isolates the anterior (front) deltoids.

1. Stand upright, knees slightly bent and shoulder width apart. Hold the dumbells at against your thighs. Your palms should be towards your body.
2. Starting with your weaker side and keeping your arm straight, raise the weight directly in front of you.

3. When your arm is parallel to the ground lower the weight slowly back to the starting position. Repeat with the other arm.
4. Avoid the tendency to arch your lower back on the last few repetitions. You will be able to handle more weight on the concentric phase (lifting the weight up) of this exercise. Make sure you can lower (eccentric phase) the dumbell under control before you progress to a higher weight

Back Dumbell Exercises

Dead lifts

Works the lower back and hamstrings. Be very careful with this exercise. If you have a history of back pain leave this one alone.

1. Stand upright, feet shoulder width apart, knees slightly bent. Hold 2 dumbells against your thighs.
2. Use your lower back to lower the weights down your leg. Your back must remain flat, the lower back arched inwards slightly. Do not round it. Keep your head up, right throughout the movement.
3. Only lower the weights as far as is comfortable even if that's only as far as your knees.
4. Stand upright using your lower back, maintaining a flat back and bent knees and keeping your head up.

Single arm row

1. Stand upright with the bench next to your left leg. Bend your left leg and rest it on the bench. Bend from your lower back and support yourself by placing your left hand on the bench. Your upper body should be parallel to the ground.

2. Hold the weight in your right hand and let it hang down so it's just off the floor. Your palm should be facing towards the bench.
3. Keeping your elbow tucked into your side raise the weight up to your midsection.
4. Slowly lower the weight to the start position and repeat. After the desired number of repetitions repeat for the other arm.

Lying bent over row

This is the same movement as the single arm row except you can work both arms at once whilst supporting your back.

1. Set the bench to a 30-45 degree incline.
2. Lie face down. Holding 2 dumbells let your arms hang down so your knuckles brush the floor. Your palms should be facing towards your feet.
3. Pull the dumbells up towards your chest and to the sides of the bench.
4. Slowly lower the weights back down and repeat.

Trapezius Dumbell Exercises

Upright row

1. Stand upright, feet shoulder width apart, knees slightly bent. Hold 2 dumbells against your thighs.
2. Keeping the weights close to your body, raise the dumbells up to your chin.
3. Hold for a count of 2 and slowly lower to the start position and repeat.

Shrugs

1. Stand upright, feet shoulder width apart, knees slightly bent. Hold 2 dumbells against your thighs.

2. Keeping your arms straight 'shrug' your shoulders as high as they will go and hold for a count of 2.
3. Relax and repeat.
4. Do not roll your shoulders backwards as you shrug up. This can cause damage to your rotator cuff muscles over time.

Biceps Dumbell Exercises

Decline seated bicep curls

1. Adjust the bench to a 45 degree incline.
2. In this 'declined' seated position hold a dumbell in either hand at your sides. Your arms should be fully extended.
3. Keep your elbows close to your body and curl the weight up.
4. Slowly lower the weight and repeat.

Hammer curls

1. Stand upright with a dumbell in either hand at your sides.
2. Turn your palms inward so they are facing your body. Your palms should be facingeach other right throughout the exercise.
3. Curl the weights up slowly keeping your elbows locked at your sides. There should be no movement from shoulder.
4. You can perform this exercise one or two arms at a time.

Preacher curls

1. Set the bench so the back rest is at approximately 45 degrees.
2. Stand behind the bench. Holding a dumbell rest the back of your upper arm on the back rest, your arm fully extended.

3. Keeping the back of your upper arm firmly against the back rest curl the weight up towards your face.
4. As you complete the curl you will notice the movement becomes easier. Slowly lower the weight until your arm is not quite fully extended and repeat for the desired number of reps before switching arms.

Concentration curls

Some dumbell exercises are difficult to describe on paper but eay when you see it. This is one of them. For now let's give it a shot.

1. Sit on the very edge of the bench with your feet flat on the floor and about 2 feet apart.
2. Holding a dumbell in your right hand place your right elbow on the inside of your right thigh, just above your knee. Support your back by placing your left hand on your left knee. Your right palm should be facing towards your left ankle.
3. From here use only your biceps to curl the weight up towards your face. Do not swing back as you lift the weight.
4. Slowly lower the weight and repeat for the desired number of reps before switching to your left arm.

Triceps Dumbell Exercises

Overhead triceps extension

1. Stand upright, feet shoulder width apart with a dumbell in your right hand.
2. Hold the weight directly above your head with your right arm fully extended. Clasp your right elbow with your left hand. Your left forearm should be infront of your face.

3. Slowly let your right elbow fold so that the weight is lowered behind your head. From this position extend your arm back to the starting position. Repeat for the desired number of reps and then switch arms.

French Press

1. Lie flat on a bench with a dumbell in either hand. Hold the weights directly above your chest with palms facing each other. The weights should be just about touching each other.
2. Keeping your shoulders locked, let your elbows fold so the weights are lowered down to either side of your head.
3. Extend both your arms back to the start position and repeat.
4. Make sure there is no shoulder movement on this exercise. The movement should come purely from your elbows.

Kickbacks

1. Stand upright with the bench next to your left leg. Bend your left leg and rest it on the bench. Bend from your lower back and support yourself by placing your left hand on the bench. Your upper body should be parallel to the ground.
2. Hold the weight in your right hand and raise your elbow so your upper arm is parallel to the ground. Your elbow should also be bent at right angles. Think of holding a pool cue ready to make a shot. In fact the movement is exactly the same...
3. Extend your elbow so now your entire arm is parallel to the ground.

4. Slowly return the weight to the start position and repeat for the desired number of reps before switching arms.

Leg Dumbell Exercises

Half squats

One of the best dumbell exercises for working the entire lower body. Works the quadriceps, hamstrings, glutes and lower back.

1. Holding a dumbell in either hand at your sides, stand upright with your feet shoulder width apart.
2. Bend from the knees until your thighs are almost parallel to the ground.
3. It is essential that you keep your back flat (not rounded), lower back slightly arched inwards and your head up.
4. Return to an upright position and repeat.

Lunges

1. Holding a dumbell in either hand at your sides, stand upright with your feet slightly less than shoulder width apart.
2. Step forward about 2 feet with your right foot. As you plant your right foot bend your right knee to about 90 degrees. Your left knee will bend automatically and should just touch the floor.
3. Push off with your right foot to return to the starting position.
4. You can alternate legs or perform all the reps on one leg at a time.

Calf Dumbell Exercises

Single leg calf raise

1. Set the back rest if the bench to an upright position. Holding a dumbell in your right hand at your side, stand upright and place your left hand on the top of the bench for support.
2. Stand on just your right leg. Rest your left foot on your right calf muscle.
3. Stand up on the tip of right toe using the bench to balance yourself. Be sure not to push yourself up with your hand, that defeats the object!
4. Slowly lower your self to the ground and repeat.

Seated calf press

1. Sit on the edge of the bench, feet flat on the floor about 12 inches apart.
2. Rest a dumbell on either thigh while you keep hold of them.
3. While staying seated raise heels by just using your toes... in effect you are standing on your tip toes while staying seated.
4. Lower your heels to the ground and repeat.

Dumbbell exercises form an integral part of most strength training programs. They can be used to develop the various different elements of strength such as maximal strength, hypertrophy or muscle mass, explosive power and strength endurance.

Free weights such as dumbbells activate smaller stabilising muscle groups to control the exercise. Resistance machines on the other hand, tend to work muscle groups in very strict planes of movement. The downside of this very strict movement is that while some muscle groups will become significantly stronger, other, smaller muscles are neglected.

The other advantage dumbbell exercises have over machines is that they fit around your body so the movement can be performed correctly. Although resistance machines can be adjusted, such as the seat height for example, the movement pattern is still largely governed by how the machine is built.

Athletes typically favor dumbbell exercises over machines as they can replicate sport-specific movements more accurately. They also know that they will develop a more balanced physique and structure if most of their routine employs free weight exercises.

The dumbbell exercises below have been divided into the major muscle groups of the body. There are literally an unlimited number of routines you can put together with just a handful of these exercises. The first step is to determine an outcome - general fitness, increased muscle mass, strength endurance, improved athletic performance for example. Not only will this dictate which dumbbell exercises you select it will also dictate the weight and number of sets and repetitions you choose. For sample weight training programs that focus on different elements of strength see the main strength training section.

Chest Dumbbell Exercises

Flat chest presses

1. Lying flat on bench, hold the dumbbells directly above chest, arms extended.
2. Lower dumbbells to chest in a controlled manner.
3. Press dumbbells back to starting position and repeat.
4. Avoid locking elbows.

Incline chest presses

1. Adjust bench to an incline of 30 to 45 degrees.

Flat chest flies

1. Lying flat on bench, hold dumbbells directly above chest.
2. Bend elbows slightly and maintain throughout the exercise.
3. Open arms to sides. Elbows should remain 'locked' in a slightly flexed position.
4. When upper arms are parallel to floor, return the weights to the starting position and repeat.

Incline chest flies

1. Adjust bench to an incline of 30 to 45 degrees.

Back Dumbbell Exercises

Dead l;ifts

1. Stand upright, feet shoulder width apart, knees slightly bent.
2. Bend lower back and knees to lower the weights down your legs. Back must remain flat, lower back should be arched inwards slightly. Keep head up throughout exercise.
3. Stand upright using lower back and legs, maintaining flat back and keeping your head up.

Single arm row

1. Stand upright next to bench. Place one knee and hand on bench. Upper body should be parallel to floor.
2. Hold one dumbbell with arm extended.
3. Raise dumbbell up to your midsection keeping back still throughout movement.
4. Slowly lower dumbbell to start position and repeat. After desired number of reps repeat for other arm.

Lying bent over rows

1. Lie face down on a flat or slightly inclined bench. Hold two dumbbells and let arms hang down.
2. Pull dumbbells up towards chest.
3. Slowly lower dumbbells back down and repeat.

Trapezius Dumbbell Exercises

Upright rows

1. Stand upright, feet shoulder width apart, knees slightly bent.

2. Keeping dumbbells close to body, raise them to chin.
3. Hold for a count of 2 and slowly lower to start position and repeat.

Shrugs

1. Stand upright, feet shoulder width apart, knees slightly bent.
2. Keeping arms straight 'shrug' shoulders as high as possible and hold for a count of 3.
3. Relax and repeat.
4. Do not roll shoulders backwards as you shrug up.

Biceps Dumbbell Exercises

Decline seated bicep curls

1. Adjust bench to a 45 degree incline.
2. Hold dumbbells at sides. Arms should be fully extended.
3. Keep elbows close to body and curl weight up by bending elblows.
4. Slowly lower dumbbells and repeat.

Hammer curls

1. Stand upright with dumbells at sides.
2. Turn palms inward so they face body.
3. Curl dumbbells up slowly keeping your elbows close to sides.

Preacher curls

1. Set bench so back rest is approx 45 degrees.
2. Stand behind the bench. Holding dumbbell rest back of upper arm on back rest, arm fully extended.

3. Keep back of upper arm against back rest and curl dumbbell up towards face.
4. Slowly lower dumbbell until arm is not quite fully extended and repeat for desired number of reps before switching arms.

Concentration curls

1. Sit on edge of bench with feet flat on the floor.
2. Holding dumbbell place elbow on inside of thigh, just above knee.
3. Curl dumbbell up towards your face. Do not swing back as you lift the weight.
4. Slowly lower the weight and repeat for desired number of reps before switching arms.

Triceps Dumbbell Exercises

Overhead triceps extensions

1. Stand upright, feet shoulder width apart.
2. Hold dumbbell directly above head with arm fully extended. Clasp elbow with free hand for support.
3. Slowly let elbow fold so dumbbell is lowered behind head.
4. Extend arm back to starting position. Repeat for the desired number of reps and switch arms.

French presses

1. Lie flat on bench. Hold dumbbells directly above chest with palms facing each other. Dumbbells should be just about touching each other.
2. Keeping your shoulders locked, let your elbows fold so dumbbells are lowered down to either side of head.

3. Extend both your arms back to start position and repeat.

Triceps Kickbacks

1. Stand upright next to bench. Place one arm and leg on bench. Upper body should be parallel to ground.
2. Holding dumbbell raise elbow so upper arm is parallel to ground. Elbow should be bent at right angles.

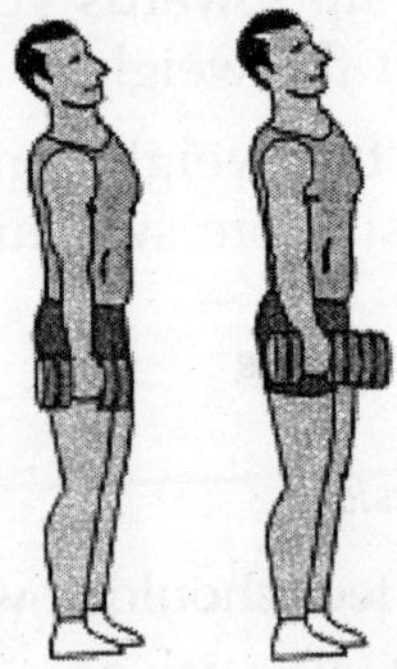

3. Extend elbow so entire arm is parallel to ground.
4. Slowly return to start position and repeat for desired number of reps before changing arms.

Leg Dumbbell Exercises

Half squats

1. Holding dumbbells at sides, stand upright with your feet shoulder width apart.
2. Bend from knees until thighs are almost parallel to the ground (avoid letting knees turn inwards).

3. Keep back flat, lower back slightly arched inwards and head up.
4. Return to upright position and repeat.

Dumbbell lunges

1. Holding dumbbells at sides, stand upright with feet slightly less than shoulder width apart.
2. Step forward about 2 feet with one foot and bend knee to about 90 degrees. As you plant your foot bend trailing knee so it nearly touches floor.
3. Push off with front foot to return to starting position.
4. Repeat for the desired number of reps and change legs.

Calf Dumbbell Exercises

Single leg calf presses

1. Set the back rest to upright position. Holding dumbbell in one hand at side, place other hand on top of bench for support.
2. Stand on one foot on edge of bench frame.
3. Stand up on tip toe using free hand to balance yourself. Do not to push yourself up with your hand.
4. Slowly lower yourself to the ground and repeat for desired number of reps before changing legs.

Seated calf raises

1. Sit on the edge of the bench, feet flat on the floor about 12 inches apart.

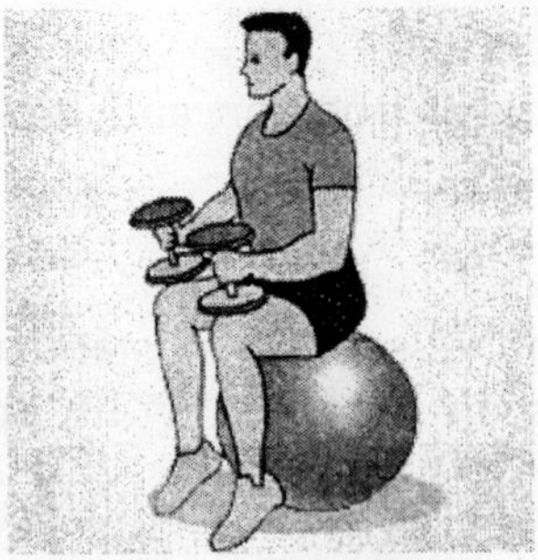

2. Rest dumbells on thighs while keeping hold of them.
3. While staying seated raise heels by just using toes.
4. Lower your heels to the ground and repeat.

4

Weight Training

Weight training programmes are designed to develop basic, functional strength. For more sample weight training programs designed to meet other objectives (such as increased muscles mass, maximal strength. A phase of basic strength training is important for adapting the body for more strenuous, subsequent weight training. It aims to balance the body's musculature by working most or all of the major muscle groups and prepares tendons, ligaments and joints helping to reduce the risk of injury later on.

Recall from the sport-specific approach to weight training programs that this basic strength phase should precede maximal strength training, hypertrophy training and explosive power training. This is important even for experienced strength-trained athletes as the nature of competitive sport places uneven stresses on the body. The basic strength phase aims to balance strength between the two sides of the body. Racket sports for example, place greater strain on the shoulder and arm muscles of one side of the body for example. Soccer players usually have a predominant kicking foot.

It also aims to restore correct balance between the flexors and extensors (such as the hamstrings and quadriceps for example). Core strength training should be a major focus of "basic strength" weight training programs. This involves working the abdominal muscles, lower back muscles and other muscle groups supporting the spinal column and hip girdle. Weak core muscles may be associated with injury, and are more likely to occur when training becomes more demanding.

Designing Weight Training Programs for Basic Strength

The length of basic strength weight training programs depends on the experience of the athlete and also the importance of strength to their particular sport. Inexperienced athletes should follow a program such as the samples below for 8-10 weeks. This helps to ensure their bodies are fully prepared for more intense training. Experienced athletes require only 3-5 weeks of basic strength training and any longer may lead to an undesirable detraining effect. However, as short as this phase may be it should not be skipped for the reasons outlined above.

Weight training programs for basic strength should be completed in the early part of the preparatory phase, often called early pre-season. However, for athletes with little or no strength training experience this basic strength phase may need to start in the off season or transition period. Because basic strength training should work most major muscle groups, a circuit training format is ideal. It alternates between muscle groups allowing a quicker recovery and a greater number of exercises to be completed. Circuit training does not have to incorporate an aerobic or cardiovascular element. It simply refers to the organization of exercises and in fact, for our purposes, a circuit training program should consist only of resistance exercises.

A wide range of equipment can be used for these circuit-style weight training programs, including bodyweight resistance bands, medicine balls, dumbbells and barbells. The parameters for resistance, sets and repetitions are covered in the table below:

Guidelines for Basic Strength training

Training Parameter	*Designer*	*Experienced*
Length of phase	8-10 weeks	3-5 weeks
Time of year	off-season	off-season
Load (fee weights)	30-40% RM	40-50% 1-RM
No. Repetitions	12-15	12-15
No. of stations per circuit	9-15	6-9
No. circuits	2-3	3-5
Duration of circuit	20-30 min	30-40 min
Rest between exercises	90sec	60 sec
Rest between circuits	23 min	12 min
Frequency per weeks	2-3	3-4

Exercises should be set up so that a muscle group is not worked on two consecutive exercises. A simple format to follow is to alternate between the upper body and lower body or total body / upper body / lower body / core exercise for example.

Inexperienced lifters should start with body weight exercises and progress to free weights. If free weights are used the resistances should start off low to moderate (see the table above) and gradually progress towards the end of the program.

Most athletes will move on to one of the maximal strength training programs following this basic strength phase. It's important that there isn't too big a jump in resistance from the end of basic strength training to the start of maximal strength training.

Sample Weight Training Programs for Basic Strength

The following sample weight training programs should follow the parameters in the table above. Exercises should be completed in the sequences set out.

Program 1 - Bodyweight exercises

— Burpees
— Push ups
— Lunges
— Crunches
— Box step up with knee drive
— Pull ups
— Alternating split squats
— Supermans

Program 2 - Medicine Balls & Resistance Bands

— Medicine ball lunge cross over
— Resistance band lateral rows
— Medicine ball oblique crunches
— Resistance band squats
— Medicine ball kneel to push ups
— Resistance band lunges
— Medicine ball reverse curls
— Resistance band bent over rows
— Medicine ball single leg chops
— Resistance band biceps curls

Program 3 - Free weights

— Dumbbell squats
— Bench presses

— V sit ups
— Deadlifts (light weight)
— Bent over rows
— Back extensions
— Lunges
— Seated dumbbell shoulder presses
— Russian twists with dumbbell
— Calf raises

The weight training programs could also be combined taking various exercises from each.

Weight Training Programs For Increasing Muscle Mass

These sample weight training programs are designed to develop increased muscle mass and lean weight. The enlargement of muscle size is known as hypertrophy and is the predominant aim of bodybuilding. While bodybuilding may still dominate many sport-specific strength training programs, in reality it is only suitable for a small number of athletes and should only make up a portion of the overall conditioning program. See the sport specific approach to strength training article to see how these sample hypertrophy weight training programs are incorporated into the annual plan.

Athletes that can benefit from a phase of hypertrophy training include shot putters, rugby players, heavyweight wrestlers and linemen in football. For these individuals, an increase in active fat-free mass is beneficial. Other athletes such as boxers and wrestlers may want to move up a weight class and can use a bodybuilding approach to do so. Traditional bodybuilding aims to increase the size of every muscle group making it a time consuming and enervating pursuit. Hypertrophy training for sport on the other hand aims only to increase the size of the prime movers, saving time and energy for other modes of training.

Whilst these hypertrophy weight training programs increase muscle and mass, they do not result in the nervous system adaptations that occur with maximal strength training - such as increased recruitment of fast twitch fibers and better synchronization of the muscles involved in the action. To this end, a phase of hypertrophy training should be followed by a phase of maximal strength training before finally being converted into sport-specific power or muscular endurance.

Designing Hypertrophy Weight Training Programs

Hypertrophy training employs moderate to heavy loads and moderate to high volume. It is generally accepted that higher volume is required to sufficiently overload the muscles to bring about substantial increases in fibre size. However, as mentioned earlier the athlete's overall training program must be taken into account - so a smaller number of exercises is used compared to traditional bodybuilding. Each session should consist of no more than 6 - 9 exercises focusing on the prime movers for 3-6 sets per exercise.

Loads should be in the 67% - 85% one repetition maximum (1RM) range so that failure in each set occurs between 6 - 12 repetitions. Sets must be performed to failure. The cumulative effect of exhaustion stimulates chemical reactions and protein metabolism so that optimal muscle growth can occur. Loads heavier than 85% 1RM, allowing less than 6 repetitions to be performed, develops maximal strength and not necessarily increased muscle mass.

Sample Hypertrophy Weight Training Programs

Hypertrophy weight training programs can follow several

formats. One popular format is the total body routine where each session consists of exercises to target all the major muscle groups in the body.

A second format perhaps more suitable for advanced lifters is a split routine in which different muscle groups are trained on different days. The simplest split routine is upper body / lower body which could be performed 4 days per week.

A similar split routine that works well is the push / pull format. Pushing exercises such as chest, shoulder and triceps lifts are performed one day and pulling exercises such as back, trapezius and bicpes lifts on another.

Which of these weight training programs is most preferable? The total body routine is usually preferred for beginners, while more advanced athletes, lifting weights at the upper end of the intensity and volume recommendations, favor one of the split routines. A phase of hypertrophy training typically lasts 4-8 weeks. However, for exceptionally long pre-seasons and where hypertrophy is particularly important (such as in football linemen), phases of hypertrophy training can be alternated with phases of maximal strength training.

Weight Training Routines For Size & Strength

These two weight training routines are designed to build muscle mass, particularly in harder gainers. Whether you want to gain size and strength for a sport such as football, or whether you simply want to gain weight, they are tried and trusted. Most weight training programs incorporate far too many exercises to develop significant size. While there are a lucky, genetically fortunate few who can train as they please, most individuals wanting to gain weight find it a struggle. If you are one these people remember "less is more".

Needless to say you are probably well aware of the importance of nutrition. Assuming you are consuming adequate calories, in the right combination of protein, carbohydrates and fats, and assuming you having the timing of your meals right, then the two weight training routines below will be highly effective.

Weight Training Routine #1

Follow this weight training program for 6-8 weeks and then schedule in a lower intensity or rest week.

Sets per exercise: 5

Reps per set: 5

Rest interval: 2-3 minutes between sets and exercises

Session 1 (Mon) - Chest, Shoulders, Triceps

— Flat barbell bench presses

— Seated dumbbell shoulder presses

— Weighted dips or narrow grip bench presses

Session 2 (Wed) - Legs, calves, Abs

— Squats or 45 degree leg presses

— Deadlifts

— Standing toes raises/calf presses

Session 3 (Thu) - Back, Traps, Biceps

— Power cleans or hang cleans

— Weighted wide grip chins or lat pull downs

— Barbell curls- Abs such as weighted crunches

Avoid training on consecutive days if possible although both these weight training routines are set up so that you can perform back-to-back sessions from time to time. You should select a weight that allows you to perform all

5 sets with 5 repetitions. The last two sets are the work sets and if you can only manage less than 4 reps in either of the two last sets, reduce the weight. Progress by increasing the weight by the smallest amount available (usually, 2.5lbs or 5kg) as soon as you complete all 5 sets at 5 reps.

Weight training routine #2

Follow this weight training program for 6-8 weeks and then schedule in a lower intensity or rest week.

— Sets per exercise: 4

— Reps per set: 6

Rest interval: 2-3 minutes between sets and exercises

Session 1

— Squats or 45 degree leg presses

— Flat barbell bench presses

— Bent over barbell rows or single arm dumbbell rows
 - Barbell curls
 - Abs such as weighted crunches

Session 2

— Seated dumbbell shoulder presses or military presses

— Deadlifts or power cleans

— Weighted Dips

— Weighted wide grip chins or lat pull downs

There are only two sessions in this weight training routine. Simply alternate the sessions every 2-3 days. This routine is flexible for those people who can't always stick to set days. It also caters for the fact that sometimes it takes you longer to recover after a session than usual.

Some isolation weight training routines such as the first routine above are simply too stressful for some people. Even if you don't feel physically tired or sore, if you're a typical hard gainer there is a chance your muscles take longer to recover and adapt to a strength session. This total body routine is less demanding on muscle groups and you may well adapt more favorably to this approach. The key is to test both weight training routines fully.

Again, when you can perform 4 sets of 6 repetitions increase the eight by the smallest amount. The last two sets are the work sets. If don't achieve at least 4-5 reps in either of these sets, reduce the weight.

Weight Training Programs For Building Maximum Strength

These sample weight training programs are designed to develop maximal strength. Training for maximal strength is not the same as training for increased muscle size known as hypertrophy training.

Only relatively few athletes require significant muscle mass and bulk whereas maximal strength is an important fitness component even for classic endurance-type sports. The sport specific approach to strength training article outlines how various types of weight training programs fit together into an overall training plan.

The main objective of maximal strength training is to increase the highest level of force an athlete can generate. Most sports require either explosive power or muscular endurance or a combination of the two. Explosive power is a combination of strength and speed. Muscular endurance is a combination of strength and endurance. It makes sense then that the greater an athlete's maximal strength is, the greater the potential for either of these fitness components.

Maximal Strength Training Over Bodybuilding

Maximal strength weight training programs are the only form of training that activates a large number of fast twitch motor units and improves muscle synchronization between the agonists and antagonists - so antagonists don't oppose the movement.

These neuromuscular adaptations plus increases in maximal strength can occur with little or no increase in muscle hypertrophy. This is important for most sports as a high strength to body mass ratio is beneficial. Although very large bodybuilders have exceptional muscle mass, their strength is not proportional to their size. Maximal strength training can result in strength gains that are up to 3x greater than the proportional gains in muscular hypertrophy. Hypertrophy is thought to result from a disturbance in the equilibrium between consumption and remanufacture of ATP. This is known as ATP deficiency theory. Maximal strength training, with its very high loads, permits only a small number of repetitions to be performed, and coupled with longer rest intervals this prevents ATP deficiency and significant hypertrophy occurring.

Designing Maximal Strength Weight Training Programs

In order to develop maximal strength, relatively heavy loads must be used - greater than 85% one repetition maximum (1RM). This permits only a small number of repetitions, between 1 and 5, per set. Maximal effort is required on each lift and as such this type of training is very taxing. Long rest intervals to allow recovery are required between sets and only a small number of exercises should make up the sessions. To further aid recovery and allow maximal effort to be performed a vertical session design is preferable to a horizontal session design. In other words, one set of each exercise should be performed in sequence and repeated rather than completing all the sets for one exercise before moving on to the next.

Even though the bar will move slowly during maximal lifts, the athlete must focus on lifting as explosively as possible in order to recruit the highest number of fast twitch motor units as quickly as possible.

Guidelines for a Maximal strength weight training programme

Load	85-100% 1RM
No. exercises	3-6
No, reps per set	1-5
No. sets per exercise	3-6
Rest interval	3-5 mins
Speed of execution	slow-medium
Frequency	2-3x week

Weight training programs designed for maximal strength development should follow a suitable period of basic strength training. Two to three sessions per week is suitable for the pre-season phase and this is often reduced to one or two maintenance sessions during the in-season.

Sample Maximal Strength Weight Training Program

While weight training programs for maximal srength are not as sport-specific as later phases of training, they should still consist of exercises that work the prime movers in the sport or event. The following program is not specific to any sport in particular and works all the major muscle groups in the body. Notice how even though the target load is +85% 1RM this is only achieved in 3 out of the 6 weeks. This stair-stepping approach of gradually increasing the load and then scheduling in a recovery week helps to prevent over-training and allows the athlete to reach a greater peak in performance.

5

Agility Exercises

The agility exercises can be used to develop speed and quickness in all kinds of sports. Along side a speed program they will help to improve your agility, speed of tought and co-ordination. They differ from traditional speed training in that they incorporate a lot more lateral movement. Most team sports and individual sports like tennis and badminton call for higg levels of agility. Agility exercises should be perfromed at the start of a session. They are not intended to be physically exhausting. They require a very high quality of work which is why they become much less effective if you have just completed a tough endurance or strength session!

Exercises

Drill 1 - Figure runs

Set out a course according to the diagram below. Cones are used to mark out a series of numbers in varying sizes. For large groups, split the team into groups of two or three and have each player run around the number or figure. Each player performs the figure once before moving onto the next figure. Soccer and hockey players can dribble a ball around the cones while football and rugby players can run with the ball to make the drill more sport-specific. Set out as many figures as you want and vary the heights so players are required to work over varying distances.

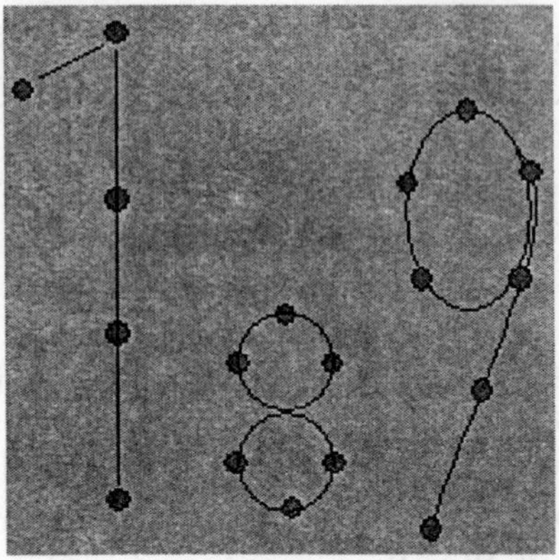

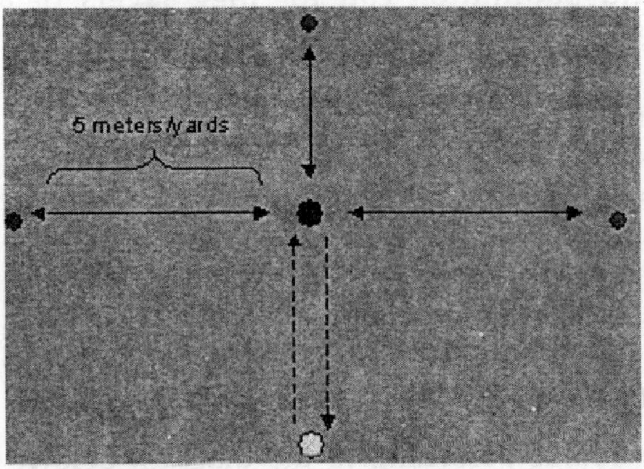

Drill 2 - agility T trill

Set up a series of cones similar to the diagram below. The working player starts by sitting down cross legged. On the start command they run to their right and back, run backwards and back an then to the left and back at full speed. A server can be added to throw a ball which the working must catch and throw back or volley back etc.

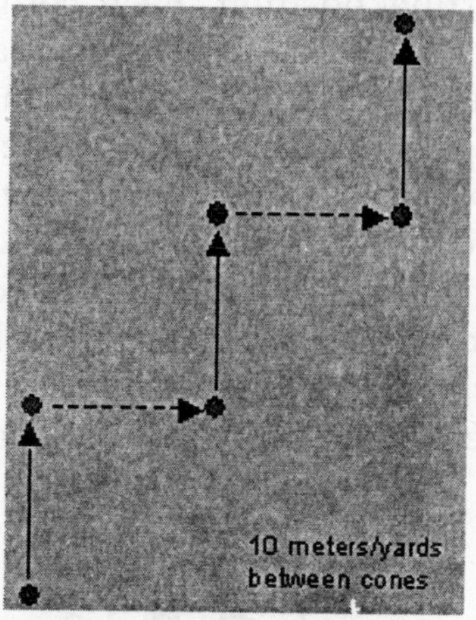

Drill 3 - Sprint lateral shuffle

Set up a series of markers similar to the diagram below. Starting at the first marker sprint to the second marker and side step to the third marker. Continue until the end. Rest and repeat in the other direction so side steps lead with opposite foot.

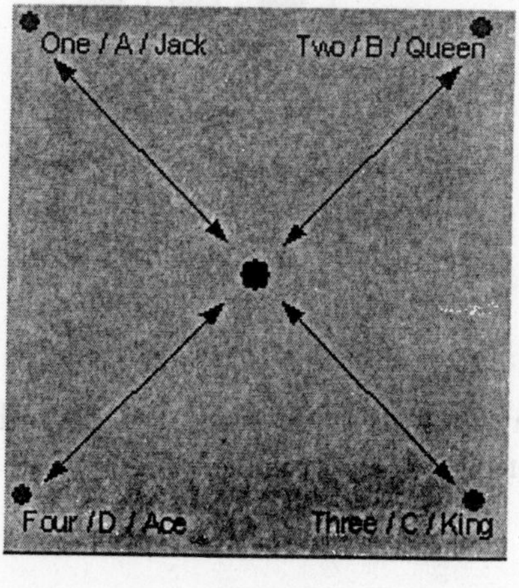

Drill 4 - Box drill

Mark out a square approximately 10 meters/yards by 10 meters/yards. Place a cone in the center of the square. This is the starting position. Each corner is given a number or name. The coach or a training partner calls out a number or name at random and you must run to the corresponding corner and return to the center. As a variation two players can use the square at once. One player is labelled A and the other B. The coach calls out two numbers. Player A must run to the corner corresponding to the first number and player B to the second number. This drill sounds complicated but it's easy to implement and it's excellent for getting players to concentrate.

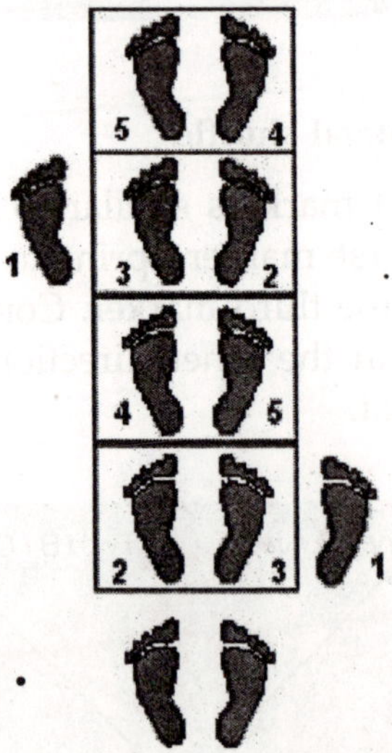

5-Count ladder drill

1. Start with your feet hip width apart at the bottom of the ladder

2. Step out to the right of the first square With your right foot immediately followed by placing your left foot into the first square.
3. Bring your right foot along side your left in the first square then step into the second square with your left foot immediately followed by the right.
4. Count these first five steps in a 1-2-3-4-5 manor.
5. Reverse the sequence by stepping out to the right of the third square with your left foot.
6. Repeat for the full length of the ladder.

Agility exercises are usually best performed in late pre-season training and during the in-season. Because they shouldn't leave you feeling tired you can perform a short, sharp agility session the day before a match or competition. This will also help to improve your mental and physical alertness as the game draws closer.

Ladder agility drills

Ladder agility drills are an excellent way to improve foot speed, agility, coordination and overall quickness.

They are an integral part of many SAQ programs and compliment many different sports and events. Speed ladder drills are about quality and form rather than producing overload. The drills are not meant to leave you fatigued or breathless in the way that shuttle runs might, for example.

It is better to perform these drills at the start of a session after the warm up. Your muscles should be fresh to ensure good quality of movement. And because they will not leave you exhausted you can perform resistance or endurance training afterwards. Here are some general guidelines for all the ladder agility drills below:

— Push off from the balls of your feet (not the toes)

— Pump your hands from shoulder height to hips (men) and from chest height to hips (women).

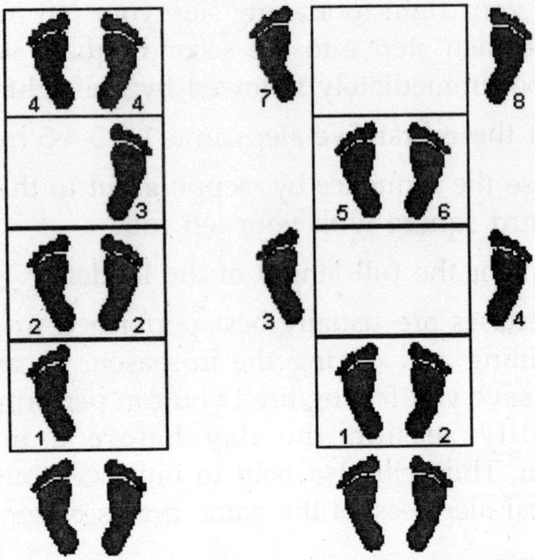

— Keep your elbows at 90 degrees at all times.

— Keep your arms, shoulders and hands relaxed.

— Try to keep your head still as much as possible.

Ladder Agility Drills

Hop scotch Drill

This is one of the simplest ladder agility drills, even for those who are too old to remember playing hop scotch (or just won't admit to it!).

— Start with your feet hip width apart at the bottom of the ladder

— Jump up with both feet and land on the left foot only in the first square

— Immediately push off with your left foot and land with both feet in the second square
— Immediately push off with both feet and land on your right foot only
— Push off from your right foot and land on both feet.
— Repeat this pattern for the full length of the ladder

In-Out Drill

Another basic drill to master but no less effective.

— Start with your feet hip width apart at the bottom of the ladder
— Step into the first square with your left foot first, immediately followed by your right foot

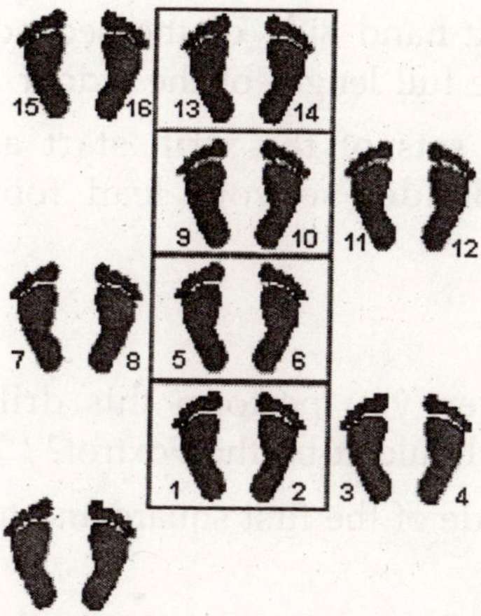

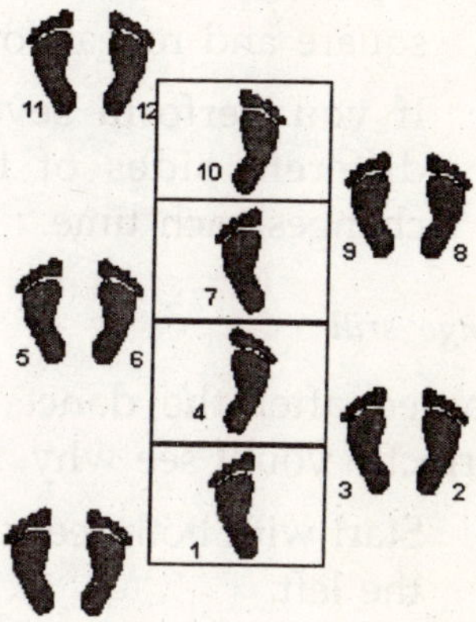

— With your left foot step outside to the left the second square, then immediately step outside the second square with your right foot
— Step back into the third square with your left foot first, followed by your right foot.
— Repeat this pattern in fluid motion for the length of the ladder

Lateral Feet Drill

The ladder agility drills from now on require more practise and greater coordination. Be sure to give yourself several dummy runs before attempting at speed.

— Start with both feet outside of the first square and to the left

— Step into the first square with your left foot first, immediately followed by your right foot... in a 1-2 motion

— Step to the right, outside the first square again with your left foot fist, followed by your right

— Now step diagonally left into the second square, with the left foot leading always keeping the same 1-2 motion

— Now step out to the left-hand side of the second square and repeat for the full length of the ladder

— If you perform several sets of this drill start at different sides of the ladder so your lead foot changes each time.

Tango srill

Named after the dance, when you perform this drill correctly you'll see why. Or should it be the Foxtrot?

— Start with both feet outside of the first square and to the left.

— Cross your left leg over your right and into the centre of the first square. Your right leg should immediately follow to the right of the first square, followed by your left leg.

— It's a 1-2-3 motion like you're dancing.

— From here your right foot comes across your left and into the centre of the second square as the pattern is repeated in the opposite direction.

— Repeat for the full length of the ladder.

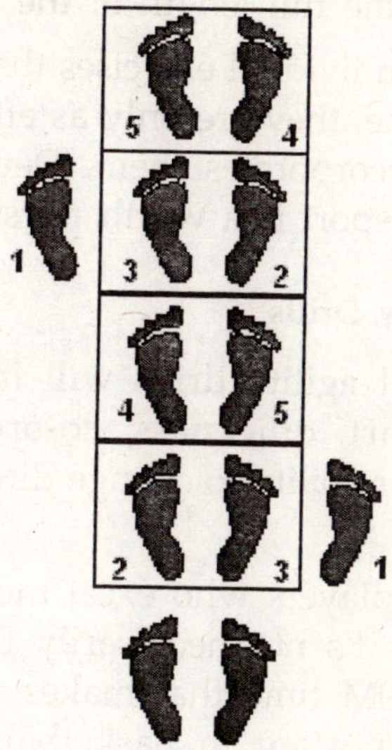

Five Count Drill

This is the most difficult to master of these ladder agility drills and requires patience even for the most dexterous. When you can perform this exercise smoothly, with speed you're ahead of most of the competition!

— Start with your feet hip width apart at the bottom of the ladder.

— Step out to the right of the first square With your right foot immediately followed by placing your left foot into the first square.

— Bring your right foot along side your left in the first square then step into the second square with your left foot immediately followed by the right.

— Count these first five steps in a 1-2-3-4-5 manor.

— Reverse the sequence by stepping out to the right of the third square with your left foot.
— Repeat for the full length of the ladder.

As with all the individual exercises that appear on this, or any other website, they are only as effective as the larger program that incorporates them. Developing speed and agility for your sport is a worth pursuit.

Basketball Agility Drills

These basketball agility drills will improve your speed around the court, quickness, co-ordination and most importantly your ability to change direction with minimal deceleration.

Basketball players who excel move with lightening-like speed. But it's not necessarily the athlete who can run a quick 100M time that makes the quickest player. Much more important in basketball is your ability to rapidly switch between forward, backward, lateral and vertical movements.

Integrating the basketball agility drills below within a speed training program can have a dramatic impact on your game. Not only will you be able to move from one end of the court to another much more quickly, you'll be able to transfer much or all of that energy into other basketball-specific movements.

Basketball Agility Drills

Agility Drill 1 - Super Shuttle

1. Starting underneath the basket with your back to the court.
2. Shuffle backwards with hands in a defensive ready position to point A.

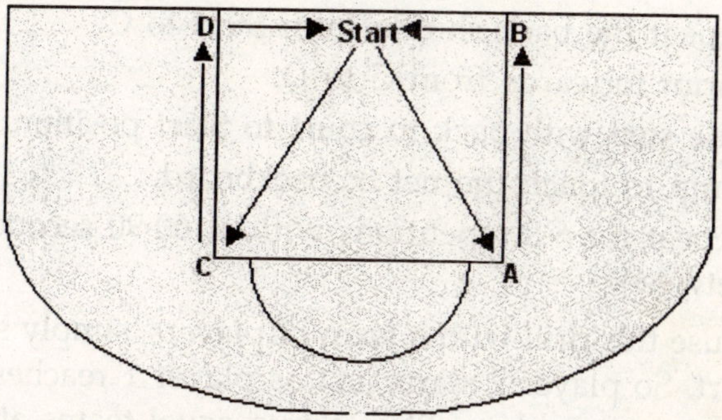

3. Sprint backwards from A to B focusing on minimising the time to change direction. 4. Side step facing the court from B to Start position (again keep hands in defensive position).

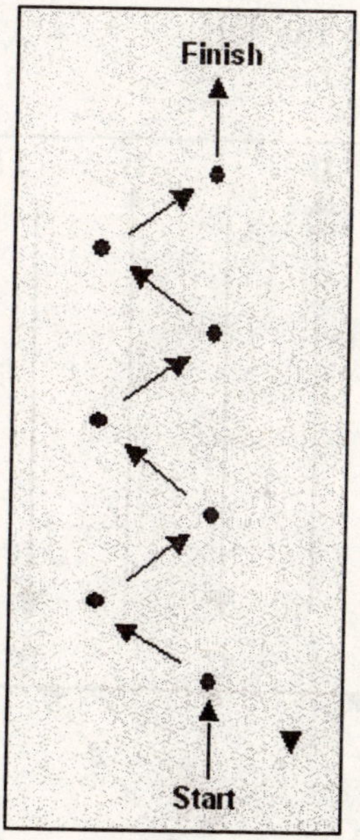

5. Jump to touch the net or backboard.
6. Repeat the back shuffle from Start to C.
7. Sprint forwards from C to D.
8. Side step with back to court to Start position.
9. Jump to touch the net or backboard.
10. Repeat for 6-8 repetitions with at 60-90 seconds rest between.

If you use this drill with a team of players, simply stagger the start. So player 2 starts just as player 1 reaches point A. The group can be split into two equal teams at either end of the court. A race makes things more interesting.

*Agility Drill 2 - **Weave in weave out***

1. Place 4 markers out in a straight line approximately 3 yards apart.
2. In between each set of markers place another marker only 3 yards to the left.

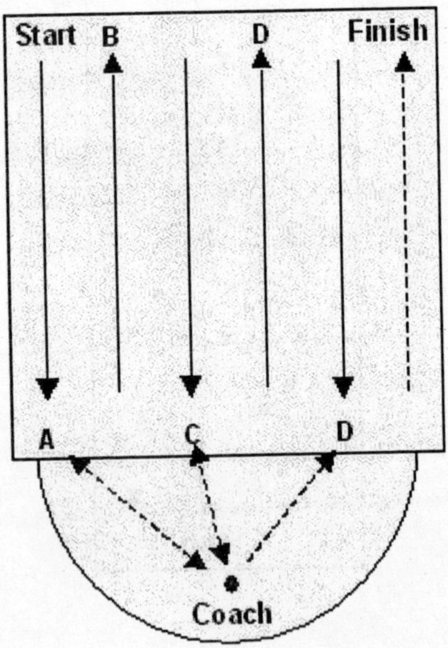

3. Sprint to marker A and then side step/shuffle to marker B leading with the left leg.

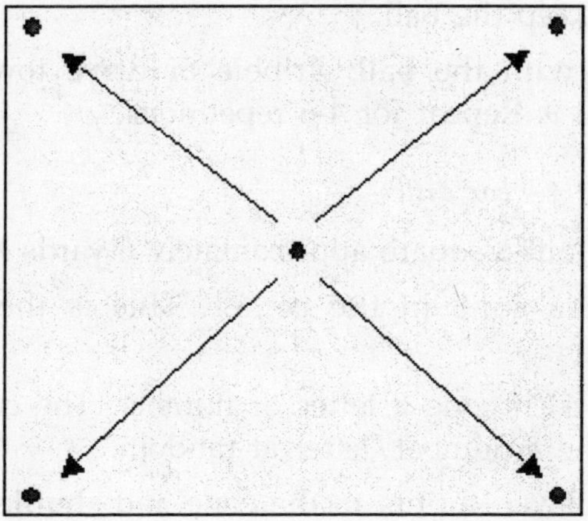

4. Side shuffle to marker C this time leading with the right leg.
5. Repeat to the finish.
6. Walk back to the start and repeat for up to 6-8 repetitions.

Agility Drill 3 - Shuttle with passes

1. Start on the baseline facing the court to the left hand side of the basket.
2. Sprint to point A and receive a pass from another player or the coach.
3. Immediately pass the ball back to the coach, turn and sprint to point B.
4. At point B, jump to touch the net or backboard.
5. On landing, turn and sprint to point C. Receive a pass and return it.

6. Turn and sprint to point D. Jump again to touch the rim or backboard.
7. Turn and sprint to pint D. Receive a pass but this time keep the ball.
8. Turn with the ball, dribble or drive towards the finish. 9. Repeat for 4-6 repetitions.

Agility Drill 4 - box drill

1. Mark out a square approximately 6 yards X 6 yards.
2. Place a cone in the center. This is the starting position.
3. Give each cone a letter or number. The coach calls out the a number/letter at random.
4. The player sprints to the cone and shuffles back to the center.
5. As soon as they arrive at the center, the coach calls another number/letter.
6. Repeat for 60-90 seconds.

With a group of players set out several boxes. Switch players every 60 seconds. Basketball agility drills like these are great for combining physical and mental awareness. It's uncanny how often players fail to remember how the cones were originally numbered when they are fatigued.

6

Plyometric Training

Athletes from a wide range of sports use plyometric training to help them reach peak physical condition. Used correctly, it can be a highly effective form of power training, especially when combined with a suitable strength training program.

Unfortunately, there is little research to define the optimal guidelines for plyometric training. While many coaches use their experience to determine the quantity and intensity of sessions, several objective guidelines have been proposed by bodies such as the National Strength & Conditioning Association and other experts in the field. It also features several sport-specific examples of plyometrics sessions as well as a range of upper and lower body animated drills.

Physiology of Plyometrics

Plyometrics refers to exercise that enables a muscle to reach maximum force in the shortest possible time. The muscle is loaded with an eccentric (lengthening) action, followed immediately by a concentric (shortening) action.

This part outlines the physiology behind how and why plyometrics works. It also examines the research that demonstrates why, as a form of power training, plyometric training is very effective. Practical guidelines for designing a plyometric training program along with animated drills can be found in the main plyometric training section

How Plyometric Exercises Work

A muscle that is stretched before a concentric contraction, will contract more forcefully and more rapidly. A classic example is a "dip" just prior to a vertical jump. By lowering the center of gravity quickly, the muscles involved in the jump are momentarily stretched producing a more powerful movement. But why does this occur? Two models have been proposed to explain this phenomenon. The first is the

Mechanical model

In this model, elastic energy is created in the muscles and tendons and stored as a result of a rapid stretch. This stored energy is then released when the stretch is followed immediately by a concentric muscle action. According to Hill the effect is like that of stretching a spring, which wants to return to its natural length. The spring is this case a component of the muscles and tendons called the series elastic component. The second model is the...

Neurophysical model

When a quick stretch is detected in the muscles, an involuntary, protective response occurs to prevent overstretching and injury. This response is known as the stretch reflex. The stretch reflex increases the activity in the muscles undergoing the stretch or eccentric muscle action, allowing it to act much more forcefully. The result is a powerful braking effect and the potential for a powerful concentric muscle action.

If the concentric muscle action does not occur immediately after the pre-stretch, the potential energy produced by the stretch reflex response is lost. (i.e. if there is a delay between dipping down and then jumping up, the effect of the counter-dip is lost). It is thought that both the mechanical model (series elastic component) and the neurophysical model (stretch reflex) increase the rate of force production during plyometrics exercises.

The Stretch-Shortening Cycle

All plyometric movements involve three phases. The first phase is the pre-stretch or eccentric muscle action. Here, elastic energy is generated and stored.

The second phase is the time between the end of the pre-stretch and the start of the concentric muscle action. This brief transition period from stretching to contracting is known as the amortisation phase. The shorter this phase is, the more powerful the subsequent muscle contraction will be.

The third and final phase is the actual muscle contraction. In practice, this is the movement the athlete desires - the powerful jump or throw.

This sequence of three phases is called the stretch-shortening cycle. In fact, plyometrics could also be called stretch-shortening cycle exercises.

How to Increase Your Vertical Jump

One very quick and simple way to demonstrate the effect of the stretch-shortening cycle is to perform two vertical jumps. During the first vertical jump the athlete bends the knees and hips (eccentric muscle action or pre-stretch) and holds the semi-squat position for 3-5 seconds before jumping up vertically (concentric contraction) as high as possible. The 3-5 second delay increases the amortisation phase.

On the second jump the athlete bends the knees and hips to the same degree but immediately jumps up without a delay. This keeps the amortisation phase to a minimum and makes best use of the stored elastic energy. The second jump will be higher.

By making use of the stretch-shortening cycle, movements can be made more powerful and explosive. Plyometrics is simply a set of drills designed to stimulate the series elastic component over and over again - preferably during movements that mimic those is the athlete's sport. But what long-term effect does practising plyometrics have on the body and performance?

A wide variety of training studies shows that plyometrics can improve performance in vertical jumping, long jumping, sprinting and sprint cycling. It appears also that a relatively small amount of plyometric training is required to improve performance in these tasks. Just one or two types of plyometric exercise completed 1-3 times a week for 6-12 weeks can significantly improve motor performance. Additionally, only a small amount of volume is required to bring about these positive changes i.e. 2-4 sets of 10 repetitions per session or 4 sets of 8 repetitions.

While upper body plyometrics has received less attention, three sessions of plyometric push ups a week has been shown to increase upper body power as measured by medicine ball throws. Using a variety of plyometric exercises such as depth jumps, counter-movement jumps, leg bounding and hopping etc., can improve motor performance. While the majority of studies have focused on untrained subjects, trained athletes such as soccer and basketball players have improved their performance with plyometrics.

Plyometrics and Concurrent Strength Training

A conditioning program consisting of both plyometric

training and resistance training can improve power performance in the vertical jump and 40yard sprint time. It appears that concurrent resistance and plyometrics training can actually improve power to a greater extent than either one alone. However, the overall program should be carefully planned as heavy weight training and plyometric training are not recommended on the same day.

Plyometrics and injury

Strength and conditioning specialists are often cautious in their prescription of plyometrics due to what they believe is an inherent risk of injury. However, there is limited data to either confirm or reject this claim.

Several researchers have explicitly stated that no injuries occurred during their plyometric studies. Most do not mention whether injuries occurred or not or to what extent.

As a precaution it has been suggested that athletes have a substantial strength training background. The criteria often cited is that the athlete should be able to back squat 1.5-2x bodyweight for lower body plyometrics and bench press 1x bodyweight for upper body plyometrics.

If injuries are more likely to occur with this form of training it may be due to improper landing, landing surface or depth jumps from too great a height. Several studies have measured the height of depth jumps on vertical jump performance. Depth jumps from both 50cm (19.7) and 80cm (31.5in) both improved power to the same extent. The same results were found between jumps of 75cm and 110cm and between jumps of 50cm and 100cm. This suggests that there may be little or no added benefits of jumping from heights above 50cm (19.7in) even though the risk of injury is likely to rise. Finally, landing surface is an important component of the plyometrics session. It should posses adequate shock absorbing properties such as grass, rubber mats and a suspended floor. Concrete, tiles, hardwood and crash mats are not suitable.

Plyometric Training for Sport Specific Power

Plyometric training has been shown to be one of the most effective methods for improving explosive power. A wide variety of athletes can benefit from power training, particularly if it follows or coincides with a strength training program. This outlines how to set up a plyometric program covering the parameters for sets, repetitions and exercise selection.

In order for plyometric training to be at its most effective it should follow a phase of maximal strength training. The purpose of plyometrics is to improve the athlete's capacity to apply more force more rapidly. Logically then, the greater the athlete's ability to generate maximal force or strength to begin with, the more of it can be converted into sport-specific power. See the sport specific approach to strength training programs for the 'big picture' and how plyometrics fits in to the overall strength program.

Plyometric Exercise Selection

There are many plyometric exercises for both the upper and lower body. As with other forms of sports training, exercise selection should mimic the movement patterns of the sport as closely as possible.

Lower body plyometric exercises

lower body plyometric exercises are suitable for many sports such as basketball, track & filed athletics, sprinting, soccer, hockey, rugby, football, baseball and so on. In fact, performance in any sport that involves jumping, sprinting or kicking can be improved with lower body plyometric exercises.

Upper body plyometric drills

Performance in sports such as basketball, volleyball, softball, baseball, tennis, badminton, golf and the throwing events in athletics can benefit with upper body plyometric exercises. Also, certain position players such as goal keepers in soccer will find these drills useful. Most upper body plyometric drills requires the use of a medicine ball.

Exercise Intensity

The intensity of plyometric exercises varies greatly. Skipping exercises are classed as low intensity, while reactive drop jumps from 32in (80cm) and above are the highest intensity of the plyometric exercises. See the table below for further intensity classifications:

Intensity of Various Plyometric Exercises

Exercise Type	Intensity
Depth jumps 32-48in (80-120cm)	High
Bounding Exercises	Submaximum
Depth jumps 8-20in (20-50cm)	Moderate
Low impact jumps/throws	Low

Plyometric training should progress gradually from lower intensity to higher intensity drills, especially for individuals who lack a significant strength training background. Increasing the load by adding additional weight thought weighted vests of ankle weights for example, is not recommended. Too great a load can reduce the speed and quality of movement negating the effects of plyometrics.

Volume

Plyometric volume relates to the number of repetitions per session. For lower body exercises a repetition is a ground contact. See the table below for the number of repetitions recommended for a plyometric training session:

Plyometric Volume Per Session	
Experience	**Ground Contacts**
Beginner	80 - 100
Intermediate	100 - 120
Advanced	120 - 140

Frequency

Typically, 2-3 sessions of plyometrics can be completed in a week. Alternatively, recovery time between sessions can be used to prescribe frequency and is recommended at 48-72 hours. It is not recommended that plyometric training be scheduled for the day after a heavy weight training session when muscles may still be sore. This poses a planning problem for athletes that may need to strength train 3-4 times per week.

The phase of the training program will also determine how many plyometric training sessions are suitable per week. For example, a track and filed athlete may require 3-4 sessions during the preparation phase reducing to 2-3 session in-season. A football player on the other hand may require only 2-3 sessions pre-season reducing to 1-2 sessions during the competitive season.

Rest Intervals

The effectiveness of a plyometric training session depends on maximal effort and a high speed of movement for each repetition. Rest intervals between repetitions and sets should be long enough to allow almost complete recovery. As much as 5-10 seconds may be required between depth jumps and a work to rest ratio of 1:10 is recommended. For example, if a set of bounds takes 30 seconds to complete, the rest interval between sets would be 300 seconds or 5 minutes.

Warming Up

As with any training an adequate warm up is required before completing a plyometric training session. The Nation Strength and Conditioning Association recommends that toe jogging and straight leg jogging be included as part of the warm up to prepare for the shock impact of plyometric drills. Plyometrics should be completed at the start of a combined session when the athlete is fresh.

Safety Considerations

Limited data exists as to whether there is any increased risk of injury through plyometric training. However, due to the stress that repeated shock-tension exercises can place on joints and connective tissue, several safety guidelines have been proposed.

It has been suggested that athletes should be able to complete a one repetition maximum squat a weight 1.5 times that of their bodyweight and bench press a weight 1-1.5 times bodyweight. Balance is also an important factor in the safe performance of plyometric exercises. Again, it has been recommended that athletes can stand on one leg for 30 seconds in order to complete less intense exercises. For more advanced exercises they should be able to stand on one leg for 30 seconds in a semi-squat position.

Plyometric training is contraindicated in prepubescent children as it may cause damage to the epithyseal plates that have yet to close. Some strength and conditioning professionals have questioned this as children routinely perform jumping movements as part of unstructured play. However, to be effective, plyometric training requires numerous, repeated maximal efforts. It is the structured nature of training that may pose an over-training risk to younger individuals. Finally, the landing surface must posses adequate shock absorbing qualities. Good choices include grass, a suspended floor and an exercise mats (not crash mats).

Sample Plyometric Training Sessions

Below are sample plyometric training sessions for badminton, basketball/volleyball and rugby. Plyometric training is one of the best ways to create incredible sport-specific power. But it must follow a well-designed program structure that will meet the demands of your sport.

Lower Body Plyometric Exercises

These animated lower body plyometric exercises can be used to develop power in any sport that involves sprinting, jumping, quick changes of direction and kicking etc. They are most effective when completed in conjunction with a suitable strength training program or following a phase of maximal strength training.

There is no evidence to suggest the risk of injury is increased during plyometric training in adults. However, as a precaution several safety guidelines have been recommended to keep plyometric exercises as safe as possible. Because plyometrics has received little scientific study compared to conventional strength training, there are no definitive guidelines regarding sets, repetitions and frequency etc. The National Strength & Conditioning Association and several leading experts in the field have proposed parameters that will help coaches and athletes design an effective training plan.

Plyometric Exercise Intensity

Not all plyometric exercises are equal in intensity. Skipping exercises for example, are relatively light while single leg bounds and depth jumps are the most intense. A program should progress gradually from lower intensity drills to more advanced plyometric exercises - particularly in an individual with less strength training experience.

The number of plyometric exercises is typically kept to a minimum also. A typical session may contain only two or three lower body plyometric exercises interspersed with upper body plyometric drills if they're appropriate for that sport.

Lower Body Plyometric Exercises (Low Intensity)

Squat jumps

1. Stand with feet shoulder-width apart, trunk flexed forward slightly with back straight in a neutral position.
2. Arms should be in the "ready" position with elbows flexed at approximately 90°.

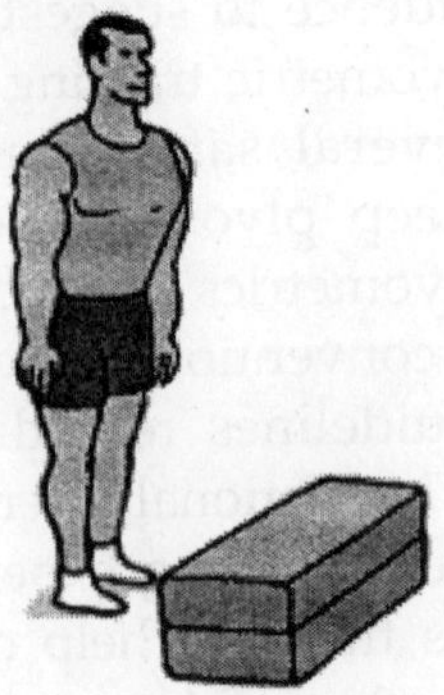

3. Lower body where thighs are parallel to ground and immediately explode upwards vertically and drive arms up. Do not hold a squat position before jumping up - keep the time between dipping down and jumping up to a minimum.
4. Land on both feet. Rest for 1-2 seconds and repeat

Prior to takeoff extend the ankles to their maximum range (full plantar flexion) to ensure proper mechanics.

Jump to box

1. Stand facing box with feet slightly wider than hip-width apart.

2. Lower body into a semi-squat position and immediately jump up onto box. Do not hold a squat position before jumping up - keep the time between dipping down and jumping up to a minimum.
3. Feet should land softly on box. Step back down (not jump back down) and repeat.

Lateral jump to box

1. Stand side on to box with feet slightly wider than hip-width apart.
2. Lower body into a semi-squat position and jump up onto box. Do not hold a squat position before jumping up - keep the time between dipping down and jumping up to a minimum.
3. Feet should land softly on box. Step back down (not jump back down) and repeat.

Lower Body Plyometric Exercises (Moderate Intensity)

Split squat jumps

1. Stand with feet hip width apart. Take left leg and step back approximately 2 feet standing on the ball of back foot.

2. Feet should be positioned at a staggered stance with head and back erect and straight in a neutral position.
3. Lower body by bending at right hip and knee until thigh is parallel to floor then immediately explode vertically.
4. Switch feet in the air so that the back foot lands forward and vice versa.

Prior to takeoff extend the ankles to their maximum range (full plantar flexion) ensure proper mechanics.

Tuck jumps

1. Stand with feet shoulder-width apart, knees slightly bent, with arms at sides.
2. Jump up bringing knees up to chest.
3. Land on balls of feet and repeat immediately.
4. Remember to reduce ground contact time by landing soft on feet and springing into air.

Lateral box push offs

1. Stand to side of box and place the left foot on top of box.

2. Push off the box using the left leg only and explode vertically as high as possible. Drive the arms forward and up for maximum height.

3. Land with right foot on the box and left foot on the ground to the other side of the box.
4. Repeat from this side.

Bounding

1. Jog into the start of the drill for forward momentum.
2. After a few feet, forcefully push off with the left foot and bring the leg forward. At same time drive your right arm forward.

3. Repeat with other leg and arm
4. This exercise is an exaggerated running motion focusing on foot push-off and air time.

Bounding with rings

1. Jog into the start of the drill for forward momentum.
2. After a few feet, forcefully push off with the left foot and bring the right leg forward. At same time swing left arm forward and land into the first ring, which is 3-4 feet out and to the left, with the right foot.
3. Continue and repeat with other leg and arm into the second ring, which is now 3-4 feet up and to the right.

4. This exercise is an exaggerated running motion focusing on foot push-off and air time.

Box drill with rings

1. Stand with feet slightly wider than hip-width apart with your body facing the first ring.
2. Hop forward using both feet and land in first ring.
3. Now hop to the left and land in the ring to the side. Now jump backwards to land in ring behind you. Finish by jumping to your right to land in final ring.
4. Rest and repeat. Remember to keep ground contact time between bounds to a minimum.Hurdle Jumps

Lateral hurdle jumps

1. Stand beside object to be cleared.
2. Bring knees up and jump vertically but also laterally off ground and over the barrier.
3. Land on both feet and immediately jump the other direction over barrier.
4. Try not to pause between jumps or sink down into a squat position.

Lower Body Plyometric Exercises (High Intensity)

Zigzag hops

1. Stand to the left of an agility ladder or similar object approximately 1-2 feet away.
2. Forcefully push off both feet and land the on the other side of the ladder.
3. Repeat and land feet back on the other side, continue repeating and so on down the ladder.4. Do not "double hop" upon each landing and keep ground contact time to a minimum.

Single leg tuck jump

This is the same as the tuck jump exercise above only one leg is used. Upon landing another jump is performed immediately with minimal ground contact time and with the same leg for the desired number of repetitions. This is repeated for the other leg after a rest period. Single leg plyometric exercises are typically more advanced and require greater strength and balance. They are suitable for sports were a takeoff is completed on one leg.

Single leg lateral hops

1. Start by standing on one leg with your hands on your waist or at your sides.
2. Proceed to hop to the side while maintaining your balance and hop back to the starting position.
3. You can place a rope on the ground or any object on the ground. The object can be small in size and height or large to increase difficulty.
4. Repeat continuously.

Depth jumps

1. Stand on box with toes close to edge, feet shoulder width apart.

2. Step off (do not jump off) box and land on both feet. Immediately jump up as high as possible and reach up with both hands towards. The jump should be vertical with no horizontal movement.

4. Ground contact time should be short unlike in the diagram. Landing should be soft.Note: Start with a box height of 30cm (12in). Intensity can be increased by gradually increasing the box height to a maximum of 107cm (42in) but this is only for experienced athletes with a substantial strength training background.

Upper Body Plyometric Drills

There are several different methods of power training. The simplest is to perform classic weight lifting exercises, such as bench presses, as explosively as possible. The problem with this method is that the barbell has to be decelerated at the end of the movement so the lifter can keep control of it. This inevitable slowing down causes a loss of power. These upper body plyometric drills allow maximum power to be generated because, unlike barbells or dumbbells, the medicine ball can be released into the air.

Racket sports such as tennis, badminton and squash, the throwing events in athletics, basketball, volleyball, rugby, and football, the martial arts and wrestling all require upper body power. Plyometric drills can be used to convert an athlete's maximal strength training into sport-specific power helping to further improve performance.

Plyometrics has not had the same level of scientific study compared to traditional strength training. As yet there are no definitive guidelines regarding volume, intensity and frequency etc. However, guidelines have been set out by leading authorities in the field.

Upper Body Plyometric Drills

Overhead throws

1. Stand with one foot in front (staggered stance) with knees slightly bent.
2. Pull medicine ball back behind head and forcefully throw ball forward as far as possible into the wall.
3. Catch ball on the bounce from the wall and repeat according to prescribed repetitions. Keep the time between pulling the ball back and starting the throw (transition phase) to a minimum. Can also be completed with a partner instead of a wall.

Side throws

1. Stand with feet hip-width apart; place left foot approximately one foot in front of right foot.
2. Hold medicine ball with both hands and arms only slightly bent.
3. Swing ball over to the right hip and forcefully underhand toss ball forward to a partner or wall. Keep the stomach drawn in to maximise proper usage of muscle.
4. Catch ball on the bounce from your partner or wall and repeat.

Over back toss

1. Stand with feet slightly wider than hip-width apart. Have a partner or trainer stand approximately 10-15 yards behind you.
2. Grasp ball and lower body into a semi-squat position. Explode up extending the entire body and throwing medicine ball up and over the body.
3. The goal is to throw the ball behind you as far as you and generating most of the power in the legs.

4. Catch ball on the bounce from your partner and repeat according to prescribed repetitions.

Slams

1. Stand with feet parallel, shoulder-width apart and knees slightly bent.
2. Pull medicine ball back behind head and forcefully throw ball down on the ground as hard as possible.
3. Catch the ball on the bounce from the ground and repeat according to prescribed repetitions.

Explosive start throws

1. Stand with feet slightly wider than hip-width apart. Knees should be slightly bent.
2. Pick medicine ball up to chest level.
3. Quickly explode up and press the ball straight out as far and fast as you can.
4. As you press the ball forward explode with either leg so that you actually sprint forward a couple of steps.

Single arm overhead throws

1. Stand with feet slightly wider than hip-width apart.
2. Grasp medicine and lower body into a semi-squat position. Explode up extending the entire body and throwing the medicine ball up into the air.
3. The aim is to throw the ball as high as you can and generating most of the power in the legs.
4. Catch ball on the bounce and repeat.

Squat throws

1. Stand with feet slightly wider than hip-width apart. Knees should be slightly bent.

2. Hold medicine ball at chest level and squat down to a parallel position.
3. Quickly explode up and jump as high as you can. As you start your jump you should start to shoulder press the ball up and reach full extensions with the arms when you are at the peak of your jump. Push ball as high as possible into the air. Try to minimise the time spent in the squatted position. It should be a quick squat and jump.
4. Catch ball on the bounce and repeat according to prescribed repetitions.

Plyometric push-ups

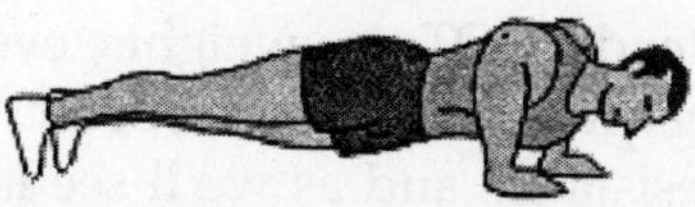

1. Start by getting into a push-up position.
2. Lower yourself to the ground and then explosively push up so that your hands leave the ground.
3. Catch your fall with your hands and immediately lower yourself into a push-up again and repeat.

Plyometrics For Soccer

Using plyometrics for soccer is one the most effective ways to increase explosive speed and power.

Research has shown that a muscle stretched before contraction will contract more forcefully and rapidly. And that is basically what plyometric exercises do...

They stretch muscles rapidly and then immediately demand a powerful concentric contraction. Let's break that last sentence down with a practical example.

Imagine the jumping movement to win a header.

The very first phase of this movement has to be a downward thrust. Try it. Try jumping off the ground without first bending your knees.

As you "dip" down just before a standing jump you are stretching muscle groups like the quadriceps and hip extensors. These are the muscles that will contract very forcefully a split second later to produce the jump. Now here's the key.

The shorter or more rapid this downward movement or pre-stretching phase is, the more forcefully those muscle groups can contract. And hence... lift off!

Can you see how general strength training like lifting heavy weights with a controlled rhythm does nothing to promote a quick pre-stretching phase?

As a side note, do NOT use weights, even light loads when performing plyometrics for soccer. Bodyweight provides ample resistance and as we'll see later, excellent form is crucial.

It's not just jumping that requires this "pre-stretching" type of movement. Any explosive movement - rapid changes in direction, sprinting (as each leg is planted on the ground) and of course, kicking, will all benefit from plyometrics for soccer.

Important Guidelines for Plyometric Training

Here are some very important guidelines to bear in mind before commencing plyometrics for soccer...

— Warm up with 5-10 minutes of light aerobic activity followed by 5-10 minutes of stretching to all major muscle groups.

— Perform plyometrics for soccer at the start of a training session before endurance training or lots of ball work. Muscles should be fresh.

- Plyometric training will not leave you out of breath or even feeling tired. Athletes often feel the urge to do more. Don't. Stick to your program to avoid injury and severe muscle soreness 34 hours later!
- Actions should be performed at high speed and with maximum intensity while maintaining high quality. For example, in jumping exercises, as your feet touch the ground you should explode upwards rapidly. Don't sink into a deep squat - minimise ground contact time.
- Two minutes rest between sets is normal. Remember, the idea is not become fatigued. Keep good form.
- Plyometrics for soccer should not contain more than 120 ground contacts for each muscle group in each session.
- Two sessions per week with 24-48 hours rest between during the late pre-season are ample. One session a week is enough during the in-season.
- It goes without saying - if any muscle feels sore during a session, end it immediately.

There is one more very important pre-condition before performing plyometrics for soccer. You must develop a solid, well-balanced strength base before you begin. Fail to do that and they can do more harm than good. If you've read some of the other articles you'll know that plyometrics converts existing strength into power. The strength has to be there initially.

Sample Plyometric Exercises for Soccer

Here are some sample plyometrics for soccer exercises. A session might contain between 10 and 15 sets of 8 to repetitions in total. For example, you could choose 4 exercises and perform 3 sets of 8 reps for each exercise.

Jump running

This is one of the easiest plyometric exercises. Simply run in 'slow motion' landing on alternate feet. Try to achieve as much height and distance with each stride as possible. For every right and left foot strike, count one repetition.

Bounding

1. Mark out a series of small cones or obstacles about 3 feet apart in a straight line. The number of obstacles depends on the number of repetitions you are performing.
2. Start behind the first obstacle in a semi squat position.
3. Jump as high and far as possible over each obstacle. It's a good idea to practise first to gauge how far apart you should set the markers. Again try to minimise ground contact time.
4. You can use anything to jump over, a training top or even just a line on a track.

Ricochets

1. Mark out a small box shape on the floor (about 2 feet square) with paint or chalk.
2. Keeping your feet together, start at one corner of the box and perform small jumps from corner to corner in a random manner.
3. For this exercise the emphasis should be on speed and rate of leg movement rather than height.
4. Each ground contact is 1 repetition.

Lateral jumps

This is an advanced plyometric exercise. Build up to it over several weeks. Keep the total number of sets for advanced exercise down to 3-6.

1. Stand alongside a bench, box or cone approximately 30cm high.
2. Keeping your feet hip distance apart jump sideways as high over the obstacle as possible.
3. Immediately jump back to the start position minimising ground contact time. This counts as one repetition.
4. You can use anything to jump over, a training top or even just a line on a track. Just make sure you discipline yourself to jump as high as possible.

Depth jumps

This is an advanced plyometric exercise. Build up to it over several weeks. Keep the total number of sets for advanced exercise down to 3-6.

1. Stand on a box, bench or sturdy chair approximately 30-40cm high.
2. Step off the bench (don't jump off) and as soon as you land explode vertically as high as you can.
3. Try to minimise ground contact time i.e. don't sink down into a deep squat before jumping up.

A Step-By-Step Guide to Using Plyometrics for soccer

Plyometrics really is one of the most effective ways to imporve speed and power - but you MUST get it right.

Plyometrics for soccer is covered in detail in "Total Soccer Fitness" — a complete soccer conditioning guide recently developed by Sport Fitness Advisor. It has already been used by coaches and players across the world to dramatically improve their (or their team's) perfromance.

Along with precise sets, reps, program design and fully illustrated exercises, it shows you precisely how to use plyometrics in a soccer conditioning plan. Of course it covers every element of fitness important in the game:

— Strength and strength endurance training
— Speed and agility training
— Aerobic and anaerobic endurance training
— Flexibility, warming up and cooling down
— Testing soccer-specific fitness
— Nutrition for soccer
— Off-season, pre-season and in-season program design

Plyometrics For Martial Arts

Plyometrics for martial arts will help to increase your explosive power, your speed and your ability to change direction quickly. On their own, plyometric drills have limited effectiveness. They are most useful when performed in conjunction with a strength training program. In fact without a strength base, plyometric training can do more harm than good.

Before performing plyometrics for martial arts you should be thoroughly warmed up. Not only will it help to prevent injury but it can also increase the effectiveness of the drills. It does this by increasing the sensitivity of the muscle spindle, which contains the fibres (called intrafusal fibres) that register the amount of stretch within a muscle.

Start with 10 minutes of aerobic exercise - jogging for example. Jogging on the toes is also often used as part of the warm up. Try to incorporate upper body movements such as arms swings and circles for example. Next perform some dynamic stretches to the upper and lower body. Kicks and leg swings make good dynamic stretches. Here are some more important guidelines when performing plyometrics for martial arts:

— Plyometrics is not recommended for anyone under the age of 16 - especially more demanding drills such as depth jumps.

— Plyometric exercises won't leave you out of breath but do not be tempted to add in more sets and repetitions.

— Perform lower body plyometric exercises on a soft surface such as grass or exercise mat.

— Two to three sessions of plyometrics per week is ample.

— Rest completely between sets for 3 to 5mins. The goal is not fatigue but to complete each repetition with the maximum amount of speed and intensity.

— A plyometric session should not contain more than 120 ground contacts for any muscle group.

— Do not add extra load such as ankle weights or a weighted vest as this can lead to injury and negatively effects the quality of the drills.

— Keep the torso erect during the movements -- it prevents undue strain on the lower back.

Plyometrics For Martial Arts - Upper Body

Plyometric push ups

1. Start by getting into a push-up position.
2. Lower yourself to the ground and then explosively push up so that your hands leave the ground.
3. Catch your fall with your hands and immediately lower yourself into a push up again and repeat.
4. Repeat for the recommended repetitions.

Single arm throws

1. Stand with feet slightly wider than hip-width apart.

2. Grasp medicine ball and lower body into a semi-squat position. Explode up extending the entire body and throwing the ball up into the air.
3. The goal is to throw the ball as high as you can and generating most of the power in the legs.
4. Catch ball on the bounce and repeat according to prescribed repetitions.

Side throws

1. Stand with feet hip-width apart; place left foot approximately one foot in front of right foot.
2. Hold medicine ball with both hands and arms only slightly bent.
3. Swing ball over to the right hip and forcefully underhand toss ball forward to a partner or wall. Keep the stomach drawn in to maximise proper usage of muscle.
4. Catch ball on the bounce from your partner or wall and repeat according to prescribed repetitions.

Slams

1. Stand with feet parallel and knees slightly bent.
2. Pull medicine ball back behind head and forcefully throw ball down on the ground as hard as possible.
3. Catch the ball on the bounce from the ground and repeat according to prescribed repetitions.

Plyometrics For Martial Arts - Lower Body

Plyometric bounding

1. Jog into the start of the drill for forward momentum.
2. After a few feet, forcefully push off with the left foot and bring the leg forward. At same time drive your right arm forward.

3. Repeat with other leg and arm.
4. This exercise is an exaggerated running motion focusing on foot push-off and air time.

Zig Zag Hops

1. Stand to the left of an agility ladder or similar object approximately 1-2 feet away.
2. Forcefully push off both feet and land the on the other side of the ladder.
3. Repeat and land feet back on the other side, continue repeating and so on down the ladder.
4. Do not "double hop" upon each landing and keep ground contact time to a minimum.

Lateral barrier jumps

1. Stand with feet slightly wider than hip-width apart with right side of body facing the barrier.
2. Hop to the right using both feet over the barrier.
3. Jump back to the start point.
4. Repeat according to the prescribed number of repetitions.

Lateral high hops

1. Stand to left side of box and place right foot on top of box.
2. Push off the box using the right leg only and explode vertically as high as possible. Drive the arms forward and up for maximum height.
3. Land with opposite foot onto box. Repeat with the other foot.
4. Repeat according to prescribed number of repetitions.

Volleyball Plyometrics Program

Volleyball plyometrics can help to increase your vertical jump and explosive power around the court. However, they should be performed alongside or following a sport-specific resistance training program.

While plyometrics is a very effective form of power training (and volleyball-specific), there are some important considerations to consider before adopting this form of conditioning into your routine.

Remember firstly that explosive power is a function of both strength and speed of muscular contraction. Volleyball plyometrics exercises will help condition your neuromuscular system to apply a greater level of force in a shorter period of time. However, if you lack basic strength, their effectiveness will be limited.

Plyometric training also places a high level of stress on joints, connective tissue and the neuromuscular system. Without a well-developed strength base, stress related injuries are much more likely to occur.

Other important guidelines relate to the amount of ground contacts in a single session, the number of sessions per week and the surface on which volleyball plyometrics are performed.

Volleyball Plyometrics Drills

The sample program consists of two volleyball plyometrics sessions per week. This is perfectly adequate to convert strength in sport-specific power and reduces the risk of over-training that can occur with more sessions each week.

Plyometrics are usually performed during the mid to late pre-season phase of training. The closed season and early pre-season can be used to develop functional and maximal strength, which is then converted to explosive power.

Because these volleyball plyometrics exercises require maximal effort and a high quality of movement, don't perform any other training immediately before - such as endurance runs, resistance training or speed training. Of course it goes without saying that a thorough warm-up should be completed first.

This routine uses a medicine ball for upper body plyometric exercises. Medicine balls are the perfect piece of equipment for developing highly specific volleyball drills. They are generally available in 1kg, 2,kg, 4kg and 5kg (2lb, 4lb, 6lb, 10lb) weights and as heavy as 10kg (20lb). Remember, for these drills to create power they must be performed explosively. If the weight is too heavy and the movement is slow then the desired training effect won't occur so stick to less than 5kg.

Drill 1 - Depth jumps

1) Stand on box with toes close to edge and facing the hoop.
2) Step off (don't jump off) box and land on both feet. Immediately jump up and reach with both hands towards the sky.

3) Ground contact time should be minimal (don't sink into the ground) and landings should be soft.

Drill 2 - Over the back toss

1) Stand with feet slightly wider than hip-width apart. Have a partner or trainer stand approximately 10-15 yards behind you.
2) Grasp ball and lower body into a semi-squat position. Explode up extending background- the entire body and throwing medicine ball up and over the head.
3) The aim is to throw the ball behind you as far as you can and generating most of the power in the legs.
4) Catch ball on the bounce from your partner and repeat according to prescribed repetitions.

Drill 3 - Lateral high hops

1) Stand to left side of box and place right foot on top of box.
2) Push off the box using the right leg only and explode vertically as high as possible. Drive the arms forward and up for maximum height.
3) Land with opposite foot onto box. Repeat with the other foot.
4) Repeat according to prescribed number of repetitions.

Drill 4 - Squat throws from chest

1) Stand with feet slightly wider than hip-width apart. Knees should be slightly bent.
2) Hold medicine ball at chest level and squat down to a parallel position.

3) Quickly explode up and jump as high as you can. As you start your jump you should throw the medicine ball as high as possible.

4) Let the ball bounce away from you rather than trying to catch it.

Drill 5 - Single arm throws

1) Stand with feet slightly wider than hip-width apart.

2) Place hand under medicine ball and lower body into a semi-squat position.

3) Explode up extending the entire body and throwing the medicine ball up into the air.

4) The aim is to throw the ball as high as you can and generating most of the power in the legs.

5) Catch ball on the bounce and repeat according to prescribed repetitions.

Drill 6 - Hurdle jumps

1) Stand 1-2 feet away from hurdle. Feet should be slightly wider than hip-width apart in a semi-squat position.

2) Driving the arms up and jump over hurdle.

3) Upon landing, quickly jump over next hurdle.

Drill 7 - Wall throws

1) Stand with one foot in front (staggered stance) or with feet together and knees slightly bent.

2. Pull medicine ball back behind head and forcefully throw ball forward as far as possible into the wall.

3. Catch ball on the bounce from the wall and repeat according to prescribed repetitions.

Drill 8 - Lateral barrier jumps

1) Stand with feet slightly wider than hip-width apart with right side of body facing the barrier.
2) Hop to the right using both feet over the barrier.
3) Jump back to the start point.
4) Repeat according to the prescribed number of repetitions.

7

Flexibility Training

Flexibility training is the most undervalued component of conditioning. While recent and ongoing debate questions its role in injury prevention, athletes can still gain much from a stretching regime. From a volleyball spike to a rugby drop kick, flexibility of the body's muscles and joints play an integral part in many athletic movements.

In general terms, flexibility has been defined as the range of motion about a joint and its surrounding muscles during a passive movement. Passive in this context simple means no active muscle involvement is required to hold the stretch. Instead gravity or a partner provides the force for the stretch.

Benefits of Flexibility Training

By increasing this joint range of motion, performance may be enhanced and the risk of injury reduced. The rationale for this is that a limb can move further before an injury occurs. Tight neck muscles for example, may restrict how far you can turn your head. If, during a tackle, your head is forced beyond this range of movement it places strain on the neck muscles and tendons.

Ironically, static stretching just prior an event may actually be detrimental to performance and offer no protection from injury. The emphasis is on "may" however, as a closer examination of the scientific literature shows that effects are often minimal and by no means conclusive.

Muscle tightness, which has been associated with an increased risk of muscle tears, can be reduced before training or competing with dynamic stretching. For this reason many coaches now favor dynamic stretches over static stretches as part of the warm up.

Competitive sport can have quite an unbalancing effect on the body. Take racket sports for example. The same arm is used to hit thousands of shots over and over again. One side of the body is placed under different types and levels of stress compared to the other. The same is true for sports like soccer and Australian rules football where one kicking foot usually predominates. A flexibility training program can help to correct these disparities preventing chronic, over-use injury.

Of course, a more flexible athlete is a more mobile athlete. It allows enhanced movement around the court or field with greater ease and dexterity. Some other benefits may include an increase in body awareness and a promotion of relaxation in the muscle groups stretched - both of which may have positive implications for skill acquisition and performance.

Types of Flexibility and Stretching

1. *Dynamic flexibility* — the ability to perform dynamic movements within the full range of motion in the joint. Common examples include twisting from side to side or kicking an imaginary ball. Dynamic flexibility is generally more sport-specific than other forms of mobility.
2. *Static Active flexibility* — this refers to the ability to stretch an antagonist muscle using only the tension

in the agonist muscle. An example is holding one leg out in front of you as high as possible. The hamstring (antagonist) is being stretched while the quadriceps and hip flexors (agonists) are holding the leg up.

3. *Static Passive flexibility* —the ability to hold a stretch using body weight or some other external force. Using the example above, holding your leg out in font of you and resting it on a chair. The quadriceps are not required to hold the extended position.

A flexibility training program can be made up of different types of stretching:

1. Dynamic stretching
2. Ballistic stretching
3. Static Active stretching
4. Static Passive stretching
5. Isometric stretching
6. PNF stretching

Which type of flexibility training is best? It depends on the sport and the athlete's outcomes - something which will be examined more closely in the articles below. As a general rule, dynamic stretches are used as part of a warm up and static stretches or PNF flexibility training is used for increasing range of motion.

Dynamic Stretching

Dynamic stretching is similar to ballistic stretching except that it avoids bouncing motions and tends to incorporate more sport-specific movements.Arms circles, exaggerating a kicking action and walking lunges (without weights) are examples of dynamic stretches. A walking lunge dynamically stretches the hip flexors by emphasizing hip extension and can reduce muscle tightness around the hip joint necessary for competition.

Dynamic stretching is useful before competition and has been shown to reduce muscle tightness. Muscle tightness is one factor associated with an increase occurrence of musculotendinous tears. More recent scientific studies seem to suggest that dynamic stretches before competition are preferably to static stretches. This may be particularly true for strength and power athletes.

Ballistic Stretching

Ballistic stretching involves active muscular effort similar to dynamic stretching. However, ballistic stretching uses a bouncing or jerking movement to increase the stretch. Ballistic stretching is effective at increasing range of motion but has been associated with injury, particularly where there has been previous injuries. Ballistic stretches often activates the muscle spindles and triggers the stretch-reflex. An example ballistic stretch is bent over toe touching with a bouncing movement. On each movement, the athlete attempts to touch the ground using gravity and bodyweight to assist in the stretch.

Static Active Stretching

Static stretching is simply the opposite of dynamic stretching. The muscle groups are stretched without moving the limb itself and the end position is held for up to 30 seconds. Static active stretching requires the strength of the opposing muscle groups to hold the limb in position for the stretch. For example, standing on one leg and holding the opposite leg out directly in front of you is classed as a static active stretch. The quadriceps actively hold the stretched limb.

Static active stretching is an effective way to increase active flexibility. A martial artist raising her leg up to an opponent's head and holding it there, is a good demonstration of static active flexibility. Being able to simply kick to head height is an example of dynamic flexibility. A static active stretch should be held for 10-30 seconds for 1-2 stretches per muscle group. As with other forms of stretching, static active stretching is not recommended before a sporting event. It may impair balance and reaction time and reduce power output and without any of the benefits of injury prevention. As part of a warm up routine, incorporate dynamic stretches, which can help reduce muscle tightness and reduce the risk of injury.

Static Stretching

Static passive stretching has been used by coaches and athletes for years without question. You may be aware of the current debate that started some years ago now, questioning whether static stretching prior to exercise really deserved the credence it has.

Static Stretches Before Performance

Once a staple part of the warm up, many strength and conditioning coaches are now suggesting that static stretches should be avoided just prior to competition. Their advice is based on a number of studies that have linked detrimental performance in power, maximal voluntary contraction, balance and reaction time tests with a static stretching routine shortly before.

However, before disregarding static stretching entirely (as a component of the warm up), it's important to take a closer look at the research. By no means have all studies found static stretches to have a negative effect on power performance. And in many studies that have found a negative association, the effects are often minimal.

Remember that this debate relates to an acute bout of static stretching prior to exercise. It is still considered important and benefical to athletes away from competition to to bring about a long-term increase in range of motion.

Long-Term Static Stretching Programs

While dynamic stretches may be more suitable as part of a warm up, static stretching is more effective at increasing range of motion. Static stretching is slow and constant and held at an end position for up to 30 seconds. Static passive stretching uses an external force to hold the stretch in position. No muscle groups are statically contracted to hold the limb in position - as they are with static active stretching.

An example is holding one leg outstretched with the heel on the floor to stretch the hamstrings. Both floor and bodyweight act as the external forces to bring about the stretch in this muscle group. Lying supine (i.e. flat on the back face up) with one leg held extended at right angles to the body (hamstring stretch) is a static active stretch. If a partner holds the leg in that position it becomes a static passive stretch.

A static stretching program effectively increases range of motion over time. This chronic adaptation may reduce the risk of injury as it increase the safe range through which a joint can be taken without injury occurring to surrounding muscles and ligaments. Perhaps most importantly, from the athlete's persepctive, regular stretching improves force production, speed and jumping ability.

Isometric Stretching Explained

One of most effective methods for improving static passive flexibility is through the use of isometric stretching. An advanced form of flexibility training that must be prescribed with caution, it is useful for developing extreme range of motion associated with martial arts for example.

Placing an outstretched leg on a chair and using your bodyweight to bring about a stretch is an example of static passive stretching. If, during the stretch, the hamstrings are contracted (i.e. trying to bend knee by pressing the heel into the chair) the activity becomes an isometric stretch.

An isometric, or static contraction occurs when tension is created in the muscle group without a change in its length. A chair, wall, the floor or a partner can act as the resistance to bring about a static contraction and isometric stretch. Aside from increasing range of motion, a second purpose of isometric stretching is to develop strength in stretched positions.

If someone with weak hip adductors attempts to see how far they can do a side split, there will come a point where their legs start to slide further and further apart. They simply don't posses the strength to hold themselves in position.

How Isometric Stretching Works

When a muscle is stretched, some muscle fibres are elongated while others will remain at rest. This is similar to the "all or none" principle of muscle contraction. The greater the stretch, the more individual fibres are stretched fully.

When a muscle, that is already in a stretched position, is subjected to an isometric contraction, additional fibres are stretched that would have otherwise remained at rest. Those resting fibres are pulled on from both ends by the muscle groups that are contracting. Fibres already in a stretched position (before the onset of the isometric contraction) are prevented from contracting by the inverse myotatic reflex and stretch to greater extent.

Isometric Stretching Guidelines

Here are the general guidelines that must be followed if isometric stretching is to be beneficial...

1. Leave 48 hours between isometric stretching routines.
2. Perform only one exercise per muscle group in a session.
3. For each muscle group complete 2-5 sets of the chosen exercise.
4. Each set should consist of one stretch held for 10-15 seconds.
5. Isometric stretching is not recommended for anyone under the age of 18.
6. If isometric stretching is to be performed as a separate exercise session, a thorough warm up consisting of 5-10 minutes of light aerobic exercise and some dynamic stretches must precede it.
7. Do not perform isometric stretching as part of a warm up or on the morning of competition. It is too intense and may adversely affect power performance.

PNF Stretching

PNF stretching (or proprioceptive muscular facilitation) is one of the most effective forms of flexibility training for increasing range of motion. PNF techniques can be both passive (no associated muscular contraction) or active (voluntary muscle contraction). While there are several variations of PNF stretching, they all have one thing in common - they facilitate muscular inhibition. It is believed that this is why PNF is superior to other forms of flexibility training.

Both isometric and concentric muscle actions completed immediately before the passive stretch help to achieve autogenic inhibition - a reflex relaxation that occurs in the same muscle where the golgi tendon organ is stimulated. Often the isometric contraction is referred to as 'hold' and the concentric muscle contraction is referred to as 'contract'.

A similar technique involves concentrically contracting the opposing muscle group to that being stretched in order to achieve reciprocal inhibition - a reflex muscular relaxation that occurs in the muscle that is opposite the muscle where the golgi tendon organ is stimulated.

Using these techniques of 'contracting', 'holding' and passive stretching results in three PNF stretching techniques. Each technique, although slightly different, involves starting with a passive stretch held for about 10 seconds.

For clarity and to compare each technique, think of a hamstring stretch in the supine (on back, face up) position for each example. The athlete places one leg extended, flat on the floor and the other extended in the air as close to right angles to the body as possible.

Hold-Relax

— A partner moves the athlete,s extended leg to a point of mild discomfort. This passive stretch is held for 10 seconds.

— On instruction, the athlete isometrically contracts the hamstrings by pushing their extended leg against their partner's hand. The partner should apply just enough force so that the leg remains static. This is the 'hold' phase and lasts for 6 seconds.

— The athlete is then instructed to 'relax' and the partner completes a second passive stretch held for 30 seconds. The athlete's extended leg should move further than before (greater hip flexion) due to autogenic inhibition activated in the hamstrings.

Contract-Relax

— A partner moves the athlete's extended leg to a point of mild discomfort. This passive stretch is held for 10 seconds.

— On instruction, the athlete concentrically contracts the hamstrings by pushing their extended leg against their partner's hand. The partner should apply enough force so that there is resistance while allowing the athlete to push their leg to the floor (i.e. through the full range of motion). This is the 'contract' phase.

— The athlete is then instructed to 'relax' and the partner completes a second passive stretch held for 30 seconds. The athlete's extended leg should move further than before (greater hip flexion) due to autogenic inhibition activated in the hamstrings.

Hold-Relax with Opposing Muscle Contraction

— A partner moves the athlete's extended leg to a point of mild discomfort. This passive stretch is held for 10 seconds.

— On instruction, the athlete isometrically contracts the hamstrings by pushing their extended leg against their partner's hand. The partner should apply just enough force so that the leg remains static. This is the 'hold' phase and lasts for 6 seconds. This initiates autogenic inhibition.

— The partner completes a second passive stretch held for 30 seconds, however the athlete is instructed to flex the hip (i.e. pull the leg in the same direction as it is being pushed). This initiates reciprocal inhibition allowing the final stretch to be greater.

Here are some other general guidelines when completing PNF stretching:

1. Leave 48 hours between PNF stretching routines.
2. Perform only one exercise per muscle group in a session.
3. For each muscle group complete 2-5 sets of the chosen exercise.
4. Each set should consist of one stretch held for up to 30 seconds after the contracting phase.
5. PNF stretching is not recommended for anyone under the age of 18.
6. If PNF stretching is to be performed as a separate exercise session, a thorough warm up consisting of 5-10 minutes of light aerobic exercise and some dynamic stretches must precede it.
7. Avoid PNF immediately before, or on the morning of competition.

Physiology of Flexibility

A number of anatomical and physiological factors influence an athlete's flexibility. While some we are stuck with (such as age, gender, and joint structure), others are under our control. These include activity level, muscle bulk and stretching exercises.

1. Joint structure

There are several different types of joint in the human body. Some intrinsically have a greater range of motion (ROM) than others. The ball and socket joint of the shoulder for example, has the greatest range of motion of all the joints and can move in each of the anatomical planes. Compare the shoulder joint to the ellipsoidal joint of the wrist. It moves primarily in the sagittal and frontal planes. The hinge joint of the ankle is similar while the modified hinge joint of the knee allows on ROM in the sagittal plane.

2. Age and Gender

ROM and flexibility decreases with age. This is due, in part to the fibrous connective tissue that takes the place of muscle fibres through a process called fibrosis. Females' tend to be more flexible than males. Older individuals should take encouragement that, just as with strength and endurance, flexibility can be increased at any age with training.

3. Connective tissue

Deep connective tissue such as fascia and tendons can limit ROM. In particular, two characteristics of connective tissue, elasticity and plasticity are related to ROM. Elasticity is defined as the ability to return to the original resting length after a passive stretch. Plasticity can be defined as the tendency to assume a new and greater length after a passive stretch.

Ligaments do not seem to display any elastic properties. However, with exposure to stretching they may extend to a new length. The strength and conditioning coach must remember that increased mobility in the ligaments reduces the stability of the joint - often an unfavorable adaptation, particularly in contact sports.

4. Muscle bulk and weight training

Hypertrophy of skeletal muscle can adversely affect ROM. It may be difficult for very bulky athletes to complete certain stretches such as an overhead triceps stretch. However, in these athletes, significant muscles mass is usually move favorable to their sport than extreme ROM. Resistance training can increase flexibility although when heavy loads are used within a limited ROM, weight training can reduce flexibility.

5. Proprioceptors

The capacity of the neuromuscular system to inhibit the antagonists (those muscles being stretched) influences flexibility. There are two important proprioceptors involved in the mechanics of stretching and flexibility. The first is the muscle spindles. Located within the muscle fibres they monitor changes in muscle length. The stretch reflex is the body's involuntary response to an external stimulus that stretches the muscle and causes a reflexive increase in muscular activity. It is the muscle spindles that activate this response.

When stretching, it is best to avoid this activating the muscle spindles and the stretch-reflex response, as it will limit motion. Static stretching does not elicit the muscle spindles, allowing muscles to relax and achieve a greater stretch.

The other important proprioceptors are the golgi tendon organs (GTO). These are located near to the musculotendinous junctions and are sensitive to increase in muscle tension. When the GTO is stimulated it causes a reflexive relaxation in the muscle. When this relaxation occurs in the same muscle that is being stretched, it is referred to as autogenic inhibition and can facilitate the stretch.

Autogenic inhibition can be induced by contracting a muscle immediately before it is passively stretched - a technique used in PNF stretching. Reciprocal inhibition occurs when the GTO is stimulated in the muscle opposite to that being stretched (i.e. so the opposing muscle relaxes). This can be achieved by simultaneously contracting the opposing muscle group to the one being passively stretched.

6. Internal environment

The athlete's internal environment affects ROM. For example, mobility is decreased immediately upon waking after a night's sleep. Ten minutes in a warm (40°C) bath increases body temperature and ROM.

7. Previous injury

Injuries to muscles and connective tissue can lead to a thickening, or fibrosing on the affected area. Fibrous tissue is less elastic and can lead to limb shortening and reduced ROM. Fibrous nodules in connective tissue and muscle are often called trigger points. A technique called myofascial release may be able to alleviate pain and restriction casued by trigger points.

Static Stretching Exercises & Flexibility Program

Stretching exercises should form an integral part of any conditioning program. Performed consistnetly, the stretching exercises below can help to do the following:

— Increase the range of motion about a joint reducing the risk of muscle and tendon tears during competitive activity.

— Relieve muscle tightness and stiffness.

— Improve postural imbalances and help to reduce chronic back pain.

— Increase localised blood flow to the muscles being stretched.

— Possibly relieve muscle soreness after intense physical activity and help to reduce the severity of DOMS (dleayed Onset Muscle Sorness).

Often seen as secondary to strength and endurance, flexibility training is neglected by many athletes. Yet stretching, both through shorter term performance enhancement and longer term injury prevention, is well worth the small amount of effort it requires.

Stretching exercises can easily be integrated into a cool down following a training session. It saves the athlete time and range of motion is increased more readily when the body is warm.

Effective Stretching

The stretching exercise below are classed as static stretches. Evidence suggests that static stretching should be avoided immediately before competition in favor of a general warm up and dynamic stretching.

1. To increase flexibility and range of motion, perform stretching exercises when the body is warm. This can be at the end of a training session or following 10 minutes of light aerobic exercise.
2. Complete a range of stretching exercises for different muscle groups. Pay particular attention to the muscle groups that are involved most in your sport.
3. Hold each stretch for 10-20 seconds. Initial tightness should gradually diminish as you hold the stretch.
4. Repeat each of the stretching exercises 2-3 times in succession.
5. Perform stretching exercises at least 3 times a week and ideally 5 times per week.
6. Ease slowly in and out of the stretch. Do not bounce! Breathe out as you stretch and continue to breathe as you hold it.
7. If you feel any pain, release the stretch immediately.

Upper And Lower Body Stretching Exercises

Shoulder stretch

Interlock your fingers and reach above your head. Your

lower back should be flat or slightly arched inwards. You can perform this exercise sitting or standing.

Triceps stretch

Place your left hand behind your head and reach as far down your back as possible. With your right hand grasp your left elbow and gently pull it behind the back of your head. You can perform this exercise sitting or standing. Repeat for the other arm.

Chest stretch

Clasp your hands behind your back. Gently straighten your elbows and raise your arms as high as comfortably possible. You can perform this exercise sitting or standing.

Lower back stretch

Lying flat on your back place the sole of your right foot on your left thigh. Grasp your right knee with your left hand and gently roll it to the left. Try to get your knee as close to the floor as possible without your right shoulder leaving the floor.

Groin stretch

Stand with your feet about 2 meters apart, toes pointing forward. Gradually shift all your weight to your right leg by bending your right knee. Your left leg stays straight. Place both your hands on your right knee for support. You can increase the starting distance between your feet for a greater stretch.

Groin stretch

Sit down and place the soles of your feet together. Clasp your ankles with your hands so that your elbows rest on your knees. Gently push your knees down with your elbows until your fell the stretch.

Quadriceps stretch

Standing upright hold onto a support with one hand (i.e. a chair) for balance. With your other hand clasp your ankle and pull your heel into your butt. Repeat for the other leg.

Hamstring stretch

Sitting down, stretch your legs out in front of you while keeping your back flat and upright. Bend your left leg keeping your left foot flat on the floor. Slowly reach forward and try to touch your right toe with both hands. Bend from your waist keeping your lower back flat and your head up. Repeat for the other leg.

Calf stretch

Stand arms length away from a wall and with feet shoulder width apart. Place your right foot about 2 feet in front of your left. Keeping both heels flat on the ground lean towards the wall by bending your right knee. Your left leg should stay straight. Push gently against the wall for a deeper stretch. Repeat for the left leg.

Achilles stretch

This is exactly the same procedure as above except as you lean towards the wall let both knees bend. Rather than leaning forward you should feel like you are lowering yourself straight down. Remember to keep both heels flat on the floor. Repeat for the other leg.

Dynamic Stretches & Stretching Routine

Dynamic stretches are best incorporated into your warm up routine before training or a competition. More recently, clinical studies have shown that traditional static stretching exercise may be detrimental to sports involving powerful movements. Dynamic stretches seem to be more effective at reducing muscle stiffness, which is thought to increase the likelihood of muscle tears. For this reason, many coaches now advocate static stretching away from competition to increase range of motion, and dynamic stretching prior to performing for injury prevention and preparation.

Some of the exercises below incorporate a stability ball. Stability balls are great for developing functional strength and core stability. They inexpensive and extremely versatile. You will find them at any store that sells exercise equipment.

Dynamic Stretches

Arm swings

1. Stand tall and hold arms out to your side.
2. Slowly swing your arms back and forth across the front of your body.
3. Repeat this continuous motion for 30 seconds.

Side sends

1. Stand with a shoulder width stance. Place a toning bar on your shoulders (optional).
2. Lean to one side keeping your torso straight. Do not bend forward or backwards.
3. Hold for a count of 2 and then repeat to the other side.
4. Complete 10 stretches each side.

Trunk rotations

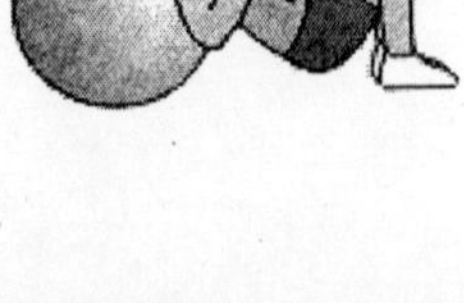

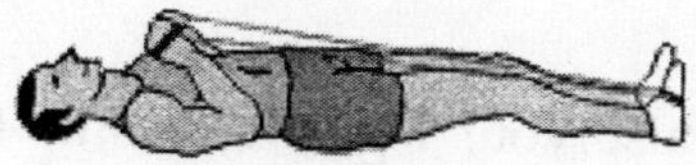

1. Stand with a shoulder width stance. Place hands on hips.
2. With knees slightly bent, turn from side to side keeping feet firmly on the floor.
3. Complete a total of 15-20 full swings.

Full back stretch

1. Lie on your back and bring both your knees to your chest with hands clasped under back of knees.
2. Roll forwards until your feet touch the floor and then immediately roll back until just before your head touches the floor.
3. Continue until you complete 10-15 full rolls.

Abdominal stretch

1. Start by lying on your back on the stability ball holding a toning bar at your chest (the toning bar is optional).
2. Push back with your feet and simultaneously push the bar over and behind your head.
3. Your legs should be straight and your arms outstretched.

4. Return to the starting position and repeat for 10-15 reps.

Hamstring stretch

1. Lie on your back and place a piece of exercise tubing (or rolled up towel) around the bottom of one of your feet.
2. Pull the tubing and raise your leg at the same time until a comfortable stretch is felt. Return to the starting position and repeat for 10-15 repetitions.
3. Repeat with other leg.

Groin stretch

1. Start by placing your right knee on top of a stability ball and maintain your balance.
2. Slowly spread your leg out to the side until you feel a stretch on the inside of your thigh.
3. Return to the start and repeat for 10-12 repetitions before changing to the other leg.

Alternate toe touches

1. Start by standing with your feet spread as far apart as comfortably possible.
2. Lean forward toward one leg and try to reach your foot or until a comfortable stretch is felt in your low back and hamstrings.

3. Now try to touch the other foot with the opposite arm. This motion should be continuous alternately touching each foot with the opposite hand.

Leg swings

1. Start by standing with your feet shoulder width apart.
2. Keeping your upper body perpendicular to the ground swing one leg forward and backward.
3. Do not swing your leg so hard that you cannot keep your upper body from moving.
4. Repeat for 10 full swings and repeat on other leg. 5. You can also swing your leg across your body stretching the abductors and adductors.

Self Myofascial Release

Self myofascial release techniques (SMRT), although not new, have become more and more prominent amongst athletes and fitness enthusiasts alike.

Both allopathic and alternative Therapists have embraced the use of myofascial release massage to reduce chronic pain and rehabilitate a range of injuries. Some therapists claim a long list of benefits, from curing tennis elbow to IBS relief. While some claims may be contentious, it seems likely that many sports men and women can benefit from this regenerative therapy. It's important to understanding two key terms in order to appreciate how self myofascial release technique acts favourably on the body. They are 'fascia' and 'trigger points'. Both are explored below before moving on to some sample self myofascial release exercises.

Fascia and Trigger Points

Fascia is a specialised connective tissue layer surrounding

muscles, bones and joints and gives support and protection to the body. It consists of three layers - the superficial fascia, the deep fascia and the subserous fascia. Fascia is one of the 3 types of dense connective tissue (the others being ligaments and tendons) and it extends without interruption from the top of the head to the tip of the toes.

Fascia is usually seen as having a passive role in the body, transmitting mechanical tension, which is generated by muscle activity or external forces. Recently, however some evidence suggests that fascia may be able to actively contract in a smooth muscle-like manner and consequently influence musculoskeletal dynamics.

Obviously, if this is verified by future research, any changes in the tone or structure of the fascia could have significant implications for athletic movements and performance. This research notwithstanding, the occurrence of trigger points within dense connective tissue sheets is thought to be correlated with subsequent injury.

Trigger points have been defined as areas of muscle that are painful to palpation and are characterised by the presence of taut bands. Tissue can become thick, tough and knoted. They can occur in muscle, the muscle-tendon junctions, bursa, or fat pad. Sometimes, trigger points can be accompanied by inflammation and if they remain long enough, what was once healthy fascia is replaced with inelastic scar tissue.

It has been speculated that trigger points may lead to a variety of sports injuries - from camps to more serious muscle and tendon tears. The theory, which seems plausible, is that trigger points compromise the tissue structure in which they are located, placing a greater strain on other tissues that must compensate for its weakness. These in turn can break down and so the spiral continues.

According to many therapists, trigger points in the fascia can restrict or alter the motion about a joint resulting in a change of normal neural feedback to the central nervous system. Eventually, the neuromuscular system becomes less efficient, leading to premature fatigue, chronic pain and injury and less efficient motor skill performance. An athlete's worst nightmare!

What causes a trigger point to form?

The list of proposed causes includes acute physical trauma, poor posture or movement mechanics, over training, inadequate rest between training sessions and possibly even nutritional factors.

Self myofascial release is a relatively simple technique that athletes can use to alleviate trigger points. Studies have shown myofascial release to be an effective treatment modality for myofascial pain syndrome, although most studies have focused on therapist-based rather than self-based treatment.

Self Myofascial Release Exercises

For these exercises you will need a foam roll (which is very inexpensive). You can get them from anywhere that sell sports medicine or physical therapy supplies.

Adductor Self Myofascial Release

1. Extend the thigh and place foam roll in the groin region with body prone (face down) on the floor.
2. Be cautious when rolling near the adductor complex origins at the pelvis.
3. If a "tender point" is located, stop rolling, and rest on the tender point until pain decreases by 75%.

Hamstring self myofascial release

1. Place hamstrings on the roll with hips unsupported.
2. Feet can be crossed so that only leg at a time is one the foam roll.
3. Roll from knee toward posterior hip.
4. If a "tender point" is located, stop rolling, and rest on the tender point until pain decreases by 75%.

Quadriceps slef myofascial release

1. Body is positioned prone (face down) with quadriceps on foam roll
2. It is very important to maintain proper core control (abdominal drawn-in position & tight gluteus) to prevent low back compensations
3. Roll from pelvic bone to knee, emphasizing the lateral (outside) thigh
4. If a "tender point" is located, stop rolling, and rest on the tender point until pain decreases by 75%.

Iliotibial band self myofascial release

1. Position yourself on your side lying on foam roll.
2. Bottom leg is raised slightly off floor.
3. Maintain head in "neutral" position with ears aligned with shoulders.
4. This may be painful for many, and should be done in moderation.
5. Roll just below hip joint down the outside thigh to the knee.
6. If a "tender point" is located, stop rolling, and rest on the tender point until pain decreases by 75%.

Upper back self myofascial release

1. Place hands behind head or wrap arms around chest to clear the shoulder blades across the thoracic wall.
2. Raise hips until unsupported.
4. Stabilise the head in a "neutral" position.
5. Roll mid-back area on the foam roll.
6. If a "tender point" is located, stop rolling, and rest on the tender point until pain decreases by 75%.

8

Endurance Training

Endurance training is quite a broad sweeping term. It's often used interchangeably with terms like "aerobic", "anaerobic", "strength" and "speed". Endurance training is important for many sports - not just the pure distance events like running, swimming and cycling for example. While the type and amount of endurance training will change according to the specific demands of the sport, even some traditional strength and power based games demand a solid aerobic base.

FACTORS AFFECTING ENDURANCE PERFORMANCE

Exercise physiology is determining the limiting factors in a particular event or activity. In endurance sports those limiting factors are based predominantly around the causes of fatigue. Unfortunately, fatigue is a complex issue and one that is likely to consist of both physical and psychological factors. However, exercise scientists have identified several major causes of exhaustion and research has shown that they can all be manipulated with proper training.

VO2 Max

It's difficult to talk about endurance performance and endurance training without mentioning VO2 max or maximal oxygen uptake. Elite endurance athletes typically have a high VO2 max and for the most part it seems to be genetically determined. However, in untrained individuals VO2 max can be improved by as much as 20%. A goal of any endurance training program is to help the athlete reach thier genetic upper limit for aerobic power. In athletes with the same or similar value for VO2 max, those who perform best tend to have a superior:

Lactate threshold

If VO2 max can be seen as an upper limit for aerobic exercise, the lacate threshold determines how much of that 'aerobic' upper limit can be used. Numerous terms have been proposed to describe the relationship between blood lactate accumulation and increasing exercise intensity and it's a subject that generates much debate. what is agreed upon is that training can have a favorable effect on lactate accumulation and when it occurs, which is associated with improved endurance performance.

Exercise economy

Two athletes may have the same VO2 max expressed in ml/kg/min and they may have the same lactate threshold expressed as a percentage of their VO2 max. Yet what is far more relevant is the speed or workload at which the athlete is exercising when they reach these two markers. Athletes with a high exercise economy expend less energy (consume less oxygen) at any given workload. As such many researchers believe economy of exercise - be it stride length, swimming technique or body position on a bicycle - is an important contributor to endurance performance.

Substrate utilisation

The oxidative energy system can utilise either fat or

carbohydrate to produce energy. However, when exercise intensity is higher (>70% VO2 max), there is a greater reliance on carbohydrate than fat for fuel. If and when carbohydrate stores are depleted exercise intensity must reduce accordingly. With training, a greater percentage of fat is used as fuel at any given work rate. This has a sparing effect on carbohydrate allowing a higher intensity to be maintained for longer.

Muscle fiber characteristics

Elite endurance athletes exhibit a high proportion of type I muscle fibers. Type I fibers have a high mitochondrial density and oxidative enzyme capacity which allows the majority of energy production to come from aerobic metabolism. While endurance training doesn't seem to change fiber types (i.e. type II fibers to type I), the metabolic characteristics of muscle fibers can be altered so that aerobic energy production becomes more efficient. Aside from these changes within skeletal muscle what other adaptations does aerobic endurance training elicit?

Other adaptations to endurance training

Following suitable training, the body becomes better able to produce ATP via aerobic metabolism. The adaptations that occur improve oxygen delivery and oxygen utilisation, increase the rate of aerobic energy production and the utilisation of fat fuel and reduce disturbances in the acid-base balance.

Aerobic Endurance Training

There are several different types of aerobic endurance training - each with a different, specific outcome and suitable for different events and sports. The duration, frequency and intensity of sessions varies with each form of training leading to different physiological adaptations within the body.

Long Slow Distance Training

As you would expect this type of training is typical of a long distance runner. Intensity is usually less than 70% VO2max, or equivalent to about 80% maximum heart rate. Duration should be near to race distance or at least 30 minutes to 2 hours long. Intensity for long, slow distance endurance training is often gauged using the "talk" test whereby the athlete can hold a conversation without being too winded.

Adaptations to this form of aerobic endurance training include improved cardiovascular and thermoregulatory function, improved mitochondrial energy production, increased oxidative capacity of skeletal muscle and increased utilisation as fat for fuel (which spares muscle glycogen). Anaerobic or lactate threshold is also likely to improve with a body better able to remove lactate. Because long distance training is low intensity (lower than competition) too great a reliance on this form of endurance running in the athlete's training program can be disadvantageous. Here is a sample training program for a marathon runner:

Sample Half Marathon Training Plan

Sunday	*Monday*	*Tuesday*	*Wednesday*	*Thursday*	*Friday*	*Saturday*
Rest	Fartlek Run (45 min)	Long Slow Distance Run (60 min)	Interval Training (45 min)	Pace/ Tempo Run (60 min)	Repetition Run (45 min)	Long Slow Distance Run (120 min)

Notice how the two long distance runs are split up with plenty of rest between? Only one run per week that approaches half marathon distance.

Pace/Tempo Training

Tempo/pace training can also be performed

intermittently or in intervals. Intensity is the same as steady state tempo/pace training except the session consists of a series of shorter bouts with brief recovery periods. It is important to keep intensity at or slightly higher than competition pace for either type of pace/tempo training. Progression should be in the form of increased duration rather than a faster running/cycling/swimming/rowing velocity etc.

Interval Training

Interval training allows the athlete to work close to their aerobic limit (VO2max) for a longer duration compared to a continuous type session. Short bouts of 3-5 minutes at an intensity close to VO2max are interspersed by periods of active recovery. Work to rest ratio should be 1:1 so a 3 minute run should be followed by 3 minutes of rest. Because this type of aerobic endurance training is very demanding, sessions should be limited both in duration and in frequency each week. Duration is usually 30-45 minutes and frequency is one or two sessions per week, with ample rest days between.

Taking the time for each 0.5km interval, allocate the same amount of time for the rest periods between. Rest should be in the form of active recovery such as brisk walking or very light jogging.

Repetition Training

This is the most intense form of aerobic endurance training. Performed at a pace greater than VO2max it places a high demand on the anaerobic energy systems. Work intervals are usually only 60-90 seconds separated by rest intervals of 5 minutes or more. Typically work to rest ratio is 1:5. Repetition training helps to improve running speed, running economy and builds a greater tolerance to lactic acid. Endurance athletes often use repetition training to help in the final kick of a race. Due to the high intensity nature, only one session per week is required.

Fartlek Training

Fartlek training combines some or all of the above aerobic endurance training techniques. A long slow run/cycle (at about 70% VO2max) form the foundation of the session and is combined with short bursts of higher intensity work. There is no set format for a Fartlek session although there are some standard sessions that have been developed by coaches over the years. Fartlek endurance training will improve VO2max, exercise economy and lactate threshold. It also adds a nice change of pace to the more monotonous steady-state training.

VO2 Max, Aerobic Power& Maximal Oxygen Uptake

VO2 max has been defined as: "the highest rate of oxygen consumption attainable during maximal or exhaustive exercise".As exercise intensity increases so does oxygen consumption. However, a point is reached where exercise intensity can continue to increase without the associated rise in oxygen consumption. To understand this in more practical terms, take a look at the Figure 1 below:

The point at which oxygen consumption plateaus defines the VO2 max or an individual's maximal aerobic capacity. It is generally considered the best indicator of cardiorespiratory endurance and aerobic fitness. However, as we'll discuss in a moment, it is more useful as an indicator of a person's aerobic potential or upper limit than as a predictor of success in endurance events.

Aerobic power, aerobic capacity and maximal oxygen uptake are all terms used interchangeably with VO2 max.

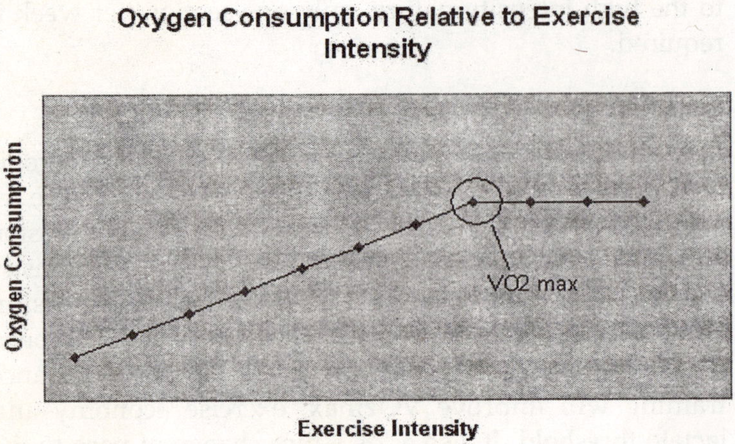

Figure 1

VO2 max is usually expressed relative to bodyweight because oxygen and energy needs differ relative to size. It can also be expressed relative to body surface area and this may be a more accurate when comparing children and oxygen uptake between sexes.

One study followed a group of 12-year-old boys through to the age of 20 - half of which were trained, the other half untrained but active. Relative to bodyweight no differences in VO2 max were found between the groups suggesting that training had no influence on maximal oxygen uptake. However, when VO2 max was expressed relative to body surface area, there was a significant difference between groups and maximal oxygen uptake did indeed increase in proportion to training.

VO2 Max In Athletes and Non Athletes

VO2 max varies greatly between individuals and even between elite athletes that compete in the same sport.

Genetics plays a major role in a person's VO2 max and heredity can account for up to 25-50% of the variance seen between individuals. The highest ever recorded VO2 max is 94 ml/kg/min in men and 77 ml/kg/min in women. Both were cross-country skiers.

Untrained girls and women typically have a maximal oxygen uptake 20-25% lower than untrained men. However, when comparing elite athletes, the gap tends to close to about 10%. Taking it step further, if VO2 max is adjusted to account for fat free mass in elite male and female athletes, the differences disappear in some studies. Cureton and Collins suggest that sex-specific essential fat stores account for the majority of metabolic differences in running between men and women.

Training & VO2 Max

In previously sedentary people, training at 75% of aerobic power, for 30 minutes, 3 times a week over 6 months increases VO2 max an average of 15-20%. However, this is an average and there are large individual variations with increases as wide ranging as 4% to 93% reported. Amongst groups of people following the same training protocol there will be responders - those who make large gains, and non-responders - those who make little or no gains. This was originally put down to a simple issue of compliance but more recent research suggests that genetics plays a role in how well any one individual responds to an endurance training program.

The extent by which VO2 max can change with training also depends on the starting point. The fitter an individual is to begin with, the less potential there is for an increase and most elite athletes hit this peak early in their career. There also seems to be a genetic upper limit beyond which, further increases in either intensity or volume have no effect on aerobic power. This upper limit is thought to be reached within 8 to 18 months.

Crucially, once a plateau in VO2 max has been reached further improvements in performance are still seen with training. This is because the athlete is able to perform at a higher percentage of their VO2 max for prolonged periods. Two major reasons for this are improvements in anaerobic threshold and running economy. Resistance training and intense 'burst-type' anaerobic training have little effect on VO2 max. Any improvements that do occur are usually small and in subjects who had a low level of fitness to begin with. Resistance training alone does not increase VO2 max even when short rest intervals are used between sets and exercises.

Considerable training is required to reach the upper limit for VO2 max. However, much less is required to maintain it. In fact peak aerobic power can be maintained even when training is decreased by two thirds. Runners and swimmers have reduced training volume by 60% for a period of 15-21 days prior to competition (a technique known as tapering) with no loss in VO2 max.

VO2 Max as a Predictor of Performance

In elite athletes, VO2 max is not a good predictor of performance. The winner of a marathon race for example, cannot be predicted from maximal oxygen uptake. Perhaps more significant than VO2 max is the speed at which an athlete can run, bike or swim at VO2 max. Two athletes may have the same level of aerobic power but one may reach their VO2 max at a running speed of 20 km/hr and the other at 22 km/hr.

While a high VO2 max may be a prerequisite for performance in endurance events at the highest level, other markers such as lactate threshold are more predictive of performance. Again, the speed at lactate threshold is more significant than the actual value itself. Think of VO2 max as an athlete's aerobic potential and the lactate threshold as the marker for how much of that potential they are tapping.

Factors Affecting VO2 Max

There are many physiological factors that combine to determine VO2 max but which of these are most important? Two theories have been proposed:

Utilisation theory

This theory maintains that aerobic capacity is limited by lack of sufficient oxidative enzymes within the cell's mitochondria. It is the body's ability to utilise the available oxygen that determines aerobic capacity. Proponents of this theory point to numerous studies that show oxidative enzymes and the number and size of mitochondria increase with training. This is coupled with increased differences between arterial and venous blood oxygen concentrations (a-vO2 difference) accounting for improved oxygen utilisation and hence improved VO2max.

Presentation theory

Presentation theory suggests that aerobic capacity is limited not predominantly by utilisation, but by the ability of the cardiovascular system to deliver oxygen to active tissues. Proponents of this theory maintain that an increase in blood volume, maximal cardiac output and better perfusion of blood into the muscles account for the changes in VO2max with training.

So what plays the greater role in determining an athlete's VO2 max - their body's ability to utilise oxygen or supply oxygen to the active tissues? Saltin and Rowell concluded that it is oxygen supply that is the major limiter to endurance performance. Studies have shown only a weak relationship between an increase in oxidative enzymes and an increase in VO2 max. One of these studies measured the effects of a 6-month swim training program on aerobic function. While oxidative enzymes continued to increase until the end, there was no change in VO2 max in the final 6 weeks of the program.

Determining VO2 Max

VO2 max can be determined through a number of physical evaluations. These tests can be direct or indirect. Direct testing requires sophisticated equipment to measure the volume and gas concentrations of inspired and expired air. There are many protocols used on treadmills, cycle ergometers and other exercise equipment to measure VO2 max directly. Indirect testing is much more widely used by coaches as it requires little or no expensive equipment. There are many indirect tests used to estimate VO2 max. Some are more reliable and accurate than others but none are as accurate as direct testing. Examples include the multistage shuttle run (bleep test), 12 minute walk test and 1.5 mile run.

VO2 Max at Altitude

VO2 max decreases as altitude increases above 1600m (5249ft) or about the altitude of Denver, Colorado. For every 1000m (3281ft) above that, maximal oxygen uptake decreases further by approximately 8-11%. Anyone with a VO2 max lower than 50 ml/kg/min would struggle to survive at the summit of Everest without supplemental oxygen.

The decrease is mainly due to a decrease in maximal cardiac output. Recall that cardiac output is the product of heart rate and stroke volume. Stoke volume decreases due to the immediate decrease in blood plasma volume. Maximal heart rate may also decrease and the net effect is that less oxygen is "pushed" from the blood into the muscles.

Effects of Aging on VO2 Max

VO2 max decreases with age. The average rate of decline is generally accepted to be about 1% per year or 10% per decade after the age of 25. One large cross sectional study found the average decrease was 0.46 ml/kg/min per year in men (1.2%) and 0.54 ml/kg/min in women (1.7%). However, this deterioration is not necessarily due to the aging process. In some cases the decease may be purely a reflection of increased body weight with no change in absolute values for ventilation of oxygen. Recall, that VO2 max is usually expressed relative to body weight. If this increases, as tends to happen with age, and aerobic fitness stays the same then VO2 max measured in ml/kg/min will decrease.

Usually, the decline in age-related VO2 max can be accounted for by a reduction in maximum heart rate, maximal stoke volume and maximal a-vO2 difference i.e. the difference between oxygen concentration arterial blood and venus blood.

Can training have an affect on this age-related decline? Vigorous training at a younger age does not seem to prevent the fall in VO2 max if training is ceased altogether. Elite athletes have been shown to decline by 43% from ages 23 to 50 (from 70 ml/kg/min to 40 ml/kg/min) when they stop training after their careers are over. In some cases, the relative decline is greater than for the average population - as much as 15% per decade or 1.5% per year.

However in comparison, master athletes who continue to keep fit only show a decrease of 5-6% per decade or 0.5-0.6% per year. When they maintain the same relative intensity of training, a decrease of only 3.6% over 25 years has been reported and most of that was attributable to a small increase in bodyweight. It seems that training can slow the rate of decline in VO2 max but becomes less effective after the age of about 50.

The Lactate Threshold

If VO2 max is your 'aerobic endurance potential' then your lactate threshold plays a significant role in how much of that potential you are tapping. Lactate threshold has been defined as: "The point during exercise of increasing intensity at which blood lactate begins to accumulate above resting levels, where lactate clearance is no longer able to keep up with lactate production.".

During low intensity exercise, blood lactate remains at or near to resting levels. As exercise intensity increases there comes a break point where blood lactate levels rise sharply. Researchers in the past have suggested that this signifies a significant shift from predominantly aerobic metabolism to predominantly anaerobic energy production. Several terms have been used to describe this shift and many coaches and athletes believe it is the same phenomenon:

— Lactate threshold
— Anaerobic threshold
— Aerobic threshold
— Onset of blood lactate accumulation (OBLA)
— Maximal lactate steady state

Although these terms are used interchangeably, they do not describe the same thing. Lactate accumulation only determines the balance between lactate production and its clearance and suggests nothing about the availability or lack of oxygen so the terms 'aerobic' and 'anaerobic' become a bit misleading. The reasons for lactate accumulation are complex and varied and not yet fully understood.

OBLA

At a slightly higher exercise intensity than lactate threshold a second increase in lactate accumulation can be seen and is often referred to as the onset of blood lactate accumulation or OBLA. OBLA generally occurs when the concentration of blood lactate reaches about 4mmol/L. The break point that corresponds to lactate threshold can often be hard to pinpoint and so some Exercise Physiologists often prefer using OBLA.

Maximal lactate steady state

Maximal lactate steady state is defined as the exercise intensity at which maximal lactate clearance is equal to maximal lactate production. Maximal lactate steady state is considered one of the best indicators of performance perhaps even more efficient than lactate threshold.

Lactate Threshold as a Percentage of VO2 Max

The lactate threshold is normally expressed as a percentage of an individual's VO2 max. For example, if VO2 max occurs at 24 km/h on a treadmill test and a sharp rise in blood lactate concentration above resting levels is seen at 12 km/h then the lactate threshold is said to be 50% VO2 max.

In theory, an individual could exercise at any intensity up to their VO2 max indefinitely. However, this is not the case even amongst elite athletes. As the exercise intensity draws closer to that at VO2 max, a sharp increase in blood lactate accumulation and subsequent fatigue occurs - the lactate threshold is broken. In world-class athletes lactate threshold typically occurs at 70-80% VO2 max. In untrained individual's it occurs much sooner, at 50-60% VO2 max. Generally, in two people with the same VO2 max, the one with a higher lactate threshold will perform better in continuous-type endurance events.

Although both Athlete 1 and Athlete 2 reach VO2 max at a similar running speed, Athlete 1 has a lactate threshold at 70% and Athlete 2 has a lactate threshold at 60%. Theoretically, Athlete 1 can maintain a pace of about 7.5 mph (12 km/h) compared to Athlete 2's pace of about 6.5 mph (10.5km/h). VO2 max has been used to predict performance in endurance events such as distance running and cycling but the lactate threshold is much more reliable. Race pace has been closely associated with lactate threshold.

Lactate Threshold and Training

With training, lactate threshold as a percentage of VO2 max can be increased. Even if there are no improvements in maximal oxygen uptake, increasing the relative intensity or speed at which lactate threshold occurs will improve performance.

Following training, the reductions in lactate concentration at any given intensity may be due to a decrease in lactate production and an increase in lactate clearance. However, Donovan and Brooks suggest that endurance training affects only lactate clearance rather than production.

Blood lactate levels after an intense exercise bout are also lower following training. For example, immediately after a 200m swim at a fixed pace, blood lactate may be as high as 13-14 mmol/L. Following 7 months of training these levels can decrease to under 4mmol/L. Before training, a swim leading to such high levels of lactate would force the swimmer to slow down dramatically or stop after the 200m. But following training, lactate levels of under 4mmol/L would probably allow the swimmer to continue after 200m, at the same pace, indefinitely.

How To Determine Lactate / Anaerobic Threshold

There are several methods used to determine an athlete's lactate or anaerobic threshold. While the most accurate and reliable is through the direct testing of blood samples during a graded exercise test, this is often inaccessible to most performers. There are several field tests that can also be used to estimate lactate threshold. They vary in their reliability but some offer an acceptable alternative for most amateur athletes.

Several terms such as onset of blood lactate accumulation and maximal lactate steady state are used interchangeably with anaerobic threshold. Technically, they do not describe precisely the same thing. In fact, although lactate threshold and anaerobic threshold occur together under most conditions, strictly speaking even these two terms are not the same. For this part however, lactate threshold and anaerobic threshold will be used interchangeably.

It is also worth bearing in mind that blood lactate and lactic acid are not the same substance. Blood lactate production is actually thought to be beneficial to endurance performance and may delay fatigue. Nevertheless, its accumulation still remains a good marker for the onset of fatigue.

Portable Lactate Analyser

Portable lactate analysers are becoming more popular amongst coaches and athletes at all levels. A good portable analyser should have the same validity and reliability as laboratory testing equipment. The Accutrend Lactate Analyser for example, has been tested using guidelines of the European Committee for Clinical Laboratory Standards and is cleared for sports medicine use by the Federal Drug Administration in the United States.

Needless to say a portable analyser is only one half of the equation. A suitable and sport-specific exercise test is still required and selecting the most appropriate protocol takes knowledge and experience. Any physiological test is only as reliable as the tester's ability to follow a set protocol. Even when a suitable assessment has been chosen, numerous variables must be kept constant for the test to remain accurate and reliable.

Conconi Test

In 1982 Conconi et al., stated that the anaerobic threshold correlated to a deflection point in the heart rate. Essentially, heart rate and exercise intensity is linear i.e. as exercise intensity increases so will heart rate. However, Conconi et a found that in all their tested subjects, including those in a follow up test, heart rate reached a plateau at near maximal exercise intensities.

Although this is a relatively simple field test that would be useful for coaches and athletes at all levels, its accuracy has been contested by subsequent researchers. Studies have found that the deflection point or plateau in heart rate only occurs in a certain number of individuals and that when it does, it significantly overestimates directly measured lactate threshold. Conconi and co-workers themselves acknowledge this controversy and cite studies that both support and contradict their original findings.

10km Run, 30Km Cycle, 30 Min Time Trial

More experienced athletes often run a 10km race or cycle 30km race at or close to anaerobic threshold. By simulating a race in training and recording heart rate, the anaerobic threshold may be determined. Alternatively, exercising for 30 minutes at the fastest sustainable pace can be used. The key is to sustain a steady pace which is why this test is more suited to experienced athletes who can gauge how fast to set off. A heart rate monitor with split time facility is required to record heart rate at each 1-minute interval. Take the average heart rate over the final 20 minutes as the heart rate corresponding to anaerobic threshold.

Heart Rate Percentage

A very simply method for estimating the anaerobic threshold is to assume anaerobic threshold occurs at 85-90% maximum heart rate (220-age). As mentioned earlier, heart rate varies greatly between individuals and even within the same individual so this is not a reliable test.

Lactate Threshold Training

Lactate threshold training will help to improve performance times in endurance events such as distance running, cycling and swimming. As its name suggests, this form of conditioning is designed to increase the exercise intensity at which the anaerobic or lactate threshold occurs.

There is some confusion amongst coaches and athletes as to the role of blood lactate and lactic acid in the body. Central to this confusion is how it contributes to fatigue. But regardless of the underlying causes, the accumulation of blood lactate remains a good indicator for subsequent exhaustion and can predict performance in many endurance events. During submaximal exercise, lactate concentration in the plasma remains at a near resting level. As the intensity increases, there comes a point when blood lactate begins to accumulate rapidly in the blood. Some researchers contest this suggesting that no specific breakpoint or threshold exists and that lactate accumulation is continuous.

Although it is difficult to accurately measure lactate threshold outside of a laboratory setting, there are some field tests that may be worth considering in order to determine your own anaerobic threshold. You may even want to consider using a portable lactate monitor and testing kit, which have become much less expensive in recent years.

There is a substantial body of research that shows training at or close to the lactate threshold increases the intensity at which it occurs. Recall that lactate threshold is often expressed as a percentage of VO2 max. For example, if an athlete reaches VO2 max at a running speed of 24km/h (15mph) and lactate begins to accumulate at 16 km/h (10mph), they are said to have a lactate threshold of 67%. World-class endurance athletes typically have thresholds of up to 90% VO2 max compared to 50% in untrained individuals.

Lactate Threshold Training Sessions

Threshold training can be either continuous or intermittent in nature. Both require an exercise intensity at or slightly above the lactate threshold. One of the most common ways to gauge lactate threshold training intensity is to monitor heart rate. While, a very quick and simple method is to simply assume your lactate threshold will occur at 85-90% of your maximum heart rate, this method lacks accuracy and reliability for many athletes. If you do want to determine training intensity this way, use the Karvonen formula rather than simply deducting your age from 220.

A more reliable method is to determine your heart rate at the lactate threshold and then to train at this heart rate intensity. This is by no means flawless however, especially as heart rate often tends to rise slowly over prolonged exercise periods without increases in intensity - a phenomenon known as cardiac drift. Cyclists can use a power meter to determine the work rate at lactate threshold and thus a suitable intensity for lactate threshold training sessions. Here is a typical interval lactate threshold training session:

Interval Training Session

Frequency	2x week
Intensity	95-105% LT
No. intervals	3-5
Interval time	10mins
Rest intervals	2-3mins

And here is a sample continuous lactate threshold training session:

Continuous Training Session

Frequency	2x week
Intensity	95-105% LT
Time	20-30mins

Interval Training For Sport Specific Endurance

Interval training can be best described as bouts of exercise interspersed with short rest intervals. It is based on the concept that more work can be completed at a higher relative intensity compared to continuous-type training. The intensity and duration of the work intervals and the length of the rest periods dictates the training response. Very short, all-out bouts of work coupled with longer rest periods are used for speed and speed endurance development. Short, very intense work intervals with short rest periods will predominantly tax the fast glycolytic energy system. Conversely, longer, lower intensity exercise bouts and short rest intervals can be used to develop aerobic endurance.

Very short rest intervals are associated with high levels of blood lactate accumulation. This effects neuromuscular control and can negatively impact speed development. Because speed training requires maximal effort and a high quality of work, longer rest periods are more appropriate to allow the athlete to recover between work intervals. In order to enhance aerobic endurance and increase VO2max towards its upper, genetic limit, interval training should consist of 3-5 minute work bouts with a 1:1 work to rest ratio or less. The intensity should equate to 90-100% VO2max. This would be suitable for endurance events such as distance running, swimming, rowing or cycling for example. It could also be used for endurance development in multi-sprint sports such as rugby.

Interval Training is Suitable for Many Sports

Nearly all athletes require a basic level of cardiovascular endurance, if for no other reason than recovery between intense bouts of work. Traditionally, coaches have opted for long, slow, distance training at 70-80% maximum heart rate. The problem with this approach is that is not specific to many sports such as the multi-sprint games and can actually be detrimental to strength and power performance. Research shows that long, slow continuous training can actually decrease anaerobic / glycolytic enzyme activity.

For sports such as basketball, soccer, hockey, tennis, rugby and so on, interval training may be more appropriate than continuous running because it can increase aerobic power and improve cardiorespiratory endurance without the associated detrimental effects on anaerobic power. However, it's not only multi-sprint sports that can benefit from interval training.

9

Baseball Training

At the highest level, baseball training revolves around strength conditioning, speed training and flexibility training. Major league players also use plyometrics and Olympic lifts to increase their upper and lower body power. But in days gone by physical training was seen an unnecessary adjunct to practise and many coaches even perceived strength conditioning as detrimental to fine motor skills required by their players.

Modern day baseball players are superb athletes. Professional players tend to be lean (body fat percent of 8-9%) and quick (under 7 seconds in the 60yard run). As for strength training, studies have shown that baseball-specific program can significantly increase batting speed and striking power as well as throwing velocity.

Power training can increase a baseball player's speed and agility. It may also improve throwing and batting velocity over and above conventional weight training. Shoulder injuries are a particular concern in baseball. Pitching (the overhand throw in particular) places an inordinate amount of stress on the shoulder complex. While strength conditioning can help to prevent such injuries, traditional weight lifting exercises may not be suitable in targeting the correct muscles or the correct movement patterns. Fortunately special exercises can be easily adopted into a baseball training program which help to significantly reduce the risk of overuse damage.

12-Month Baseball Strength Training Program

An effective baseball strength training program - one designed to significantly improve your performance - is not about bulking up. In fact: Too much size can reduce your range of motion, restrict your quickness and agility and hamper your execution of skills. But strength training for baseball is very different from bodybuilding.

The main priority for baseball players is to develop maximal strength and then convert those gains into explosive power — in particular hitting and throwing power. It's important to remember that bigger muscles are not necessarily more powerful muscles.

Of the relatively few players and coaches who incorporate strength conditioning, most take a less than efficient approach. They follow the same routine week after week, month after month always trying to lift heavier and heavier weights. And if their routine does change, it usually comes straight from a glossy fitness magazine. Not the best approach for developing outstanding baseball-specific strength.

Four Phases of a Baseball Strength Training Program

Nearly all strength training programs for sport are split into several distinct phases. Each phase has it's own objective and builds on the phase previously. So, for example, the first phase might build a solid foundation of strength, preparing the body for more strenuous training down the line. Another phase might focus on developing maximal strength or muscle bulk. The phase following that might aim to convert strength into sport-specific power of muscular endurance.

In baseball we can split the year into these 4 phases:

— *Off-Season* — Also called the "closed season" or transition phase, when little or no competitive baseball is played

— *Early Pre-Season* — This is the period when players first return after the break. Training is typically more general and gradual eases into more intense sessions

— *Late Pre-Season* — Training should be at its most intense during the late pre-season. The aim is to peak as the competitive season begins

— *In-Season* — Training in the competitive season is about maintaining the gain developed during the pre-season. The amount of training tends to be lower to accommodate games

Splitting an annual program up like this is an example of perdioization. The 12-month program is the big picture, which can be broken down into smaller periods or phases. But periodization doesn't end there. Each phase can be split into smaller phases again (often called cycles) and the smallest cycle - the microcycle - is usually one week of training. Within each phase, each cycle and each week, the intensity and volume of training varies. Compare that to the typical bodybuilder who aims to lift heavier and heavier weights for more and more repetitions indefinitely. Don't worry if it sounds a bit overly complicated. After you've read about each phase below it becomes much clearer. Then the chart at the bottom ties everything together.

Phase 1 - Develop foundational strength

What exactly is "foundational strength"? For the purposes of this article it refers to a balanced base of strength in all major muscle groups and in particular the core region.

Foundational strength training prepares the joints, ligaments, tendons and connective tissue for more demanding training later on in the program. But not only does it prepare the body, it helps to balance it.

Any sport places uneven stresses on the body. Pitchers throw forcefully with the same arm thousands of times a year. Swinging the bat in the same direction over and over, develops muscles on one side of the body more than the other side.

Over time, small imbalances can compound into chronic over-use injuries. The most effective way to prevent this is with exercises that re-develop the natural balance between the left and right side, as well as opposing muscle groups.

In this phase, a good deal of time should be dedicated to strengthening your center of power. The muscles of the trunk and lower back connect the upper and lower body. They support every twisting, turning, jumping and lateral movement. They are literally the link through which all movement passes.

Finally, a foundational period like this is important for any level of athlete - even for seasoned weight lifters. If a player is new to weight lifting, this phase becomes doubly important and can last 8-12 weeks or more.

Phase 2 - Developing maximal strength

Once you've built a solid and well-balanced foundation, the next phase of the baseball strength training program is develop maximal strength. Maximal strength is simply defined as the most amount of weight you can lift once or 1 repetition maximum.

It's important that you devote a portion of your baseball strength program to developing maximal strength. Why? Because it serves as a foundation for muscular power and speed. But there is one condition.A weight lifter may take several seconds to lift a weight, especially towards the end of a set. That may sound like a short time but in most sporting movements it's an eternity. Imagine how much force a pitcher would generate if their throwing action lasted 10 seconds! The goal is to spend some time in the pre-season increasing your strength to a peak and then to convert that strength into explosive power just as the competitive season approaches.

The more maximal strength you have, the greater your potential for speed and power. There are some key differences between maximal strength and what's called hypertrophy training. Hypertrophy is simply the increase in muscle size that bodybuilders look for. But their type of training doesn't cause the same neurological adaptations that maximal strength training does.

Phase 3 - Conversion to Power

The stronger you are the harder you can hit, or throw right? Well not necessarily. Very few sports and events require maximal strength. Remember, strength makes no allowances for time. To accelerate quickly, pitch forcefully and hit powerfully you have to be able to apply as much of your strength as quickly as possible.

Power is a combination of strength and speed. Increase either one (without reducing the other) and you increase your explosive power. There are several training methods to increase power but they all have one element in common. The speed of the lift or movement is sharp and explosive. To allow for these quick contractions you have to reduce the amount of weight or resistance.

One very effective method for developing power is plyometric training. Very often this uses only bodyweight. For the upper body, medicine ball are used.

Phase 4 - Maintain your gains

During the competitive season, baseball strength training

can be reduced to two or even one session per week. It's good to perform a combination of maximal strength training exercises and explosive power exercises.

During the in-season, varying the training load and intensity becomes critical. Training over a week should taper off towards a game. Training as a whole should taper off towards the end of the season or leading up to a particularly important game.

In the months of the closed season it can be a good idea to have a break from strength training altogether. But keep this break no longer than 3-4 weeks. After 5 weeks most of the gains made over the previous year are lost. If you do continue to train over this period, keep it informal and unstructured. Don't pay too much attention to the number of sets and reps or the order of exercises. This is a good time to choose exercises that work neglected parts of the body.

Comprehensive Baseball Weight Training Program

This sample baseball weight training program is a continuation of the baseball strength training article. If you missed that first article be sure to take a look. It explains how to structure your training over an entire year.

Strength training for any sport is usually broken into separate phases. And in baseball the end-goal is not bulk and size or even maximal strength — the main objective is to develop explosive power. This baseball weight training program assumes you have shown correct form and technique and that you've had medical clearance from a physician. At this point you should read the disclaimer.

Phase 1 - Develop Foundational Strength

Circuit training is excellent format for this phase of a

baseball weight training program. At this stage THE most important objective is to balance and prepare the body for an excellent season. Training can be less specific to baseball but it's a good idea to incorporate some exercises that match the demands of the sport.

Time year: Early pre-season

Duration: 4-8 weeks

Days per week: 2-3 (Leave 24hrs between sessions)

Load: Bodyweight or 50-60% 1 rep max

Reps: 15-20

Circuits: 2-3

Rest interval: 30 secs between exercises

Rest interval: 2-3 mins between circuits

The last few reps on each station should be taxing. When you can comfortably perform the number of reps suggested increase the weight.

1. Squat to Presses x 12-15
2. Single Arm Dumbbell Rows x 12 (each arm)
3. Bent Knee Sit Ups x 20
4. Push-Ups x 15-20
5. Fast Feet on Box x 90 seconds
6. Barbell Upright Rows x 15
7. Supermans x 20
8. Dumbbell Forward Lunges x 10 (each leg)
9. Burpees x 15
10. Oblique Curls x 20

Phase 2 - Developing maximal strength

Training for maximum strength requires experience and a good foundation of strength. Because it includes the use of heavier weights ideally you should have someone to spot you. Do not jump straight to this phase in the baseball weight training program. It's only effective if you stay injury free and the best way to do that is to prepare and balance the body first with a foundational program - even if you're an experienced lifter.

Time year: Mid pre-season

Duration: 6 weeks

Days per week:3 (leave 24-48hrs between sessions)

Load: 80-90% 1 rep max

Reps: 4-8

Sets: 3-5

1. Squats/Leg Presses - 3sets x 6-8reps
2. Bench Presses 3sets x 6-8reps
3. Leg Curls - 3sets x 10reps
4. Dumbbell Overhead Presses 3sets x 6-8reps
5. Calf Raises - 3sets x 8-10reps
6. Wide Grip Pull Downs - 3 sets x 6-8reps
7. Weighted Crunches - 3 sets x 10-15reps

Phase 3 - Conversion to power

In this third phase of the baseball weight training program, the preparation and gains made over the previous few months are converted into baseball specific strength and power.

The movement patterns in throwing, hitting and sprinting short distances are sharp and explosive. Increased strength alone won't make a dramatic impact on your performance. Being able to apply that strength quickly will.

The emphasis now moves away from heavy, near-maximum load, to lighter resistance that you can move explosively. If the weight is too heavy, the movements will be slow and you'll fail to make the neural adaptations that are important in power development.

The program below uses someplyometric exercises. This is not the only method to develop power but it is effective. Plyometric training can be deceptively tough. It won't leave you out of breath or fatigued.

In fact you may end the sessions feeling like you need to do more. Don't! Don't compare this type of training with maximal strength training which does leave you feeling fatigued.

Time year: Late pre-season

Duration: 4 weeks

Days per week:2-3

Load: Bodyweight, medicine ball or 50-60% 1 rep max

Reps: 8-12

Sets: 2-3

1. Lateral Jumps 3 x 10 (bodyweight)
    1. Stand alongside a bench, box or cone approximately 30cm high.
    2. Keeping your feet hip distance apart jump sideways as high over the obstacle as possible.
    3. Immediately jump back to the start position minimising ground contact time. This counts as one repetition.
    4. You can use anything to jump over, a training top or even just a line on a track. Just make sure you discipline yourself to jump as high as possible.
2. Plyometric Push-Ups 3 x 10 (bodyweight)

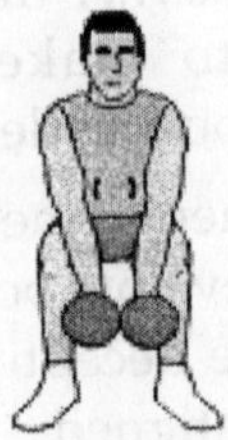

Same as a regular push-up except as you extend your arms push up explosively so your hands leave the ground. Then allow your elbows to bend slightly to absorb the shock as you land. Lower and repeat. A variation of this exercise is to quickly clap your hands as they are in the air.

3. Depth Jumps 3 x 10 (bodyweight)

   1. Stand on a box, bench or sturdy chair approximately 30-40cm high.
   2. Step off the bench and as soon as you land explode vertically as high as you can.
   3. Try to minimise ground contact time i.e. don't sink down into a deep squat before jumping up.

4. Pull Over Throw 3 x 10 (medicine ball)

   1. Lying on your back with knees bent, have your partner stand about 10 feet away.
   2. Hold a medicine ball directly over your chest with your arms extended.
   3. With your arms still extended, lower the ball behind your head as far as you can... if you can touch the floor with the ball great!
   4. From this position throw ball forward toward your feet releasing it when your arms are over your chest and abdomen.
   5. Have your partner pass the ball back to you and repeat.

5. Dumbbell Squats w/ Rotational Swings 3 x 10
    1. Start position: Holding a dumbell in each hand start in squatted position with dumbells between legs.
    2. Start movement by standing up and keeping arms straight rotate shoulders and trunk towards the left.
    3. Return to the starting position and repeat to the other side.
    4. Repeat for the prescribed number of repetitions.
6. Reverse Curls 3 x 12 (medicine ball)
    1. Start position: Lie with back on floor or bench with hips flexed at 90° and feet in air holding onto a medicine ball. Position arms at sides with palms down on floor.

    2. Leading with the heels towards the ceiling, raise glutes (butt) off floor or bench.
    3. Return to start position.
    4. Remember keep legs from swinging to prevent momentum throughout the exercise.
7. Alternating Squats w/ Press 3 x 10
    1. Start by holding a dumbbell in each hand at shoulder level.
    2. Squat down to about parallel and explode up to a standing position.

3. Once you have squatted half way up then starting pressing the dumbells over your head.
4. Use the momentum from your squat to propel the dumbells above your head. Remember to stay in control of the dumbbells at all times.

8. Side Throws 3 x 10 (medicine ball)
   1. Stand side on, with your partner about 20 feet to your left. Keeping feet shoulder width apart and knees bent place your right foot slightly in front of your left.
   2. Hold a medicine ball with both hands directly in front of you. Keep your arms extended and parallel to the floor.
   3. Swing ball as far to the right as is comfortable allowing your hips to turn with your arms. From this position.
   4. Immediately swing the ball to your left throwing the ball to your partner.
   5. Repeat for the desired number of repetitions and then repeat for the other side to complete one set.

In Season Baseball Weight training

During the competitive season the aim is to maintain both an adequate level of maximal strength and explosive power. Because it takes less to maintain a level of fitness than it does to develop it, you can cut your strength training sessions down to once or twice per week.

Avoid weight training the day before a game. You might want to perform one strength session per week and one power session. Or you could combine some of the exercises into one session per week depending on your time commitments.

10

Golf Fitness

Strength, power, flexibility, balance, core stability, body awareness, even endurance: they're all physical traits that every consistent golfer (even the fair-weather players) must possess. The golf industry is littered with gadgets and gimmicks for increasing accuracy and shot distance. Yet for all their claims and guarantees most remain independently unproven. Compare that to a basic golf fitness program.

After 5 weeks of completing 5 minutes of very simple home exercises 5 times a week, golfers increased their clubhead speed by an average of 24%. While it could be argued that clubhead speed is only one small facet of a golfer's overall game, it is highly correlated with a player's handicap. In other words, the lower a player's handicap is, the higher their clubhead speed at impact tends to be. In fact, a 24% increase relates to a reduction of 4 shots off a golfer's handicap. This is just one of several studies that proves the benefits of conditioning for golf.

And the benefits of golf fitness training are not reserved for the young. Golfers aged 55-75 have also benefited from strength and flexibility training - both in terms of general health parameters and their performance on the course.

For the more serious golfers, conditioning can no longer be seen as an unnecessary add-on to their practise routine. Just as a committed amateur athlete spends time on their technique and their fitness, so must the golfer who demands to be the best they can. There is a caveat however: In order to improve performance in any sport, training must be specific to the demands of the game involved. Of the few golfers who do appreciate the importance of physical training, most still make the mistake of following a general fitness routine. If you want hit every shot consistently further you need to take a different approach. Not a more complicated approach. Not a more time-consuming approach.

Golf Weight Training Program

The golf weight training program has been tailor made to meet the specific demands of the game. Why is strength training for golfers at every level of the game?

Increase you ability to generate power (longer shots) and just as importantly - it will help to counteract the imbalances that are inherent with swinging a club the same way thousands of times each year. Still here? Before moving on to the golf weight training program below it's important that read the disclaimer. Please don't attempt any exercise program without first seeing a health care professional. While a well-designed strength training program is one of the best ways to prevent golf-related injuries, it's NOT a good remedy is they exist already. In fact it can matters worse - again please take advice from your health care professional.

Golf Weight Training Basics

— The golf weight training program below is split into 3 phases. Each phase is simply a period of time in which you train in a particular way to achieve a particular objective. The exercises are different in each phase and build on the ones performed previously. Each phase requires only 2 sessions a week commitment.

— Warming up is essential before a round and there are scientific studies to back this up. It's also important to warm up before each golf weight training session. Perform 5-10 minutes of light aerobic exercise (jogging, stationery bike, cross trainer etc.) and then do some stretches to all the major muscle groups.

— Some of the exercises below are unique and you may not be familiar with them. It's important to master correct technique and you can only do this by first using very light weights. Spend at least a session of two becoming familiar with the exercises without resistance.

— It goes without saying that if any of the exercises cause you pain or discomfort you should stop them immediately.

— Sets and repetitions are indicated below. To make gains in strength you have to overload your muscles above and beyond what they are comfortable with. That means the last few sets should be difficult. If a target of 10 repetitions is set and you can perform 12 with ease, the weight is too light. Similarly, if you can only perform 6-8, the weight is too heavy and you need to decrease the resistance.

— Each routine below is performed twice per week. But avoid training on back-to-back days. In fact ideally leave at least two days between golf weight training sessions. You should also avoid strength training the day before a competition or important 18 holes.

Phase 1 - Build a solid foundation

The off-season (usually winter) when you play no competitions and less golf, is the ideal time to start your golf weight training program. Of course, the timing may not fit and it's better to make a start now than to wait until next year. Remember though, whatever point your are in the year, always start with this phase.

The exercises in this phase of the golf weight training program are more conventional and use moderate weights. At this stage THE most important goal is prepare the body for more demanding sessions later on. It's also a time to address some of the imbalances inherent in many golfers.

The session is set up in as a Circuit. This simply means you perform one set of each exercise in succession with minimal rest between exercises. Here are the parameters for the circuit training routine that makes up phase 1.

— Time of Year: Off-season/winter months

— Phase length: 8 weeks

— No. sessions: 2 x week

— No. exercises: 10

— Resistance: 50% 1 repetition maximum

— Repetitions: 15-20

— No. circuits: 2-3

— Rest between exercises: 30 secs

— Rest between circuits: 2-3 mins

— Speed of lifts: Smooth and controlled

And here are the exercises:

1. Push-ups x 15-20
2. Alternating Squats with Press x 15

3. Lat Pull Downs (wide grip) x 15
4. Oblique Crunches x 20
5. Dumbbell Lunges x 10 (each leg)
6. Barbell Upright Rows x 15
7. Reverse Flyes x 15
8. Dumbbell Curls x 15
9. Back Extensions on Stability Ball x 20
10. Barbell Reverse Wrist Curls x 15-20

Phase 2 - *Develop golf-specific power*

Once you've built a solid foundation of strength, it's time to convert those gains into explosive power. The golf swing is a powerful movement - power being a combination of strength and speed. Just becoming stronger won't necessarily allow you to hit the ball further. Becoming stronger and then developing the ability to apply that strength quickly is the real key. That's how you'll increase club head speed and that's how you'll hit the ball farther.

The exercises below should be performed explosively. On the contraction or the difficult part of the lift, aim to move the weight as quickly and forcefully as possible. Slowly lower the weight to the start position and repeat. Do not lock joints out at any stage. Always keep a degree of flexion in the elbows or knees for example. Instead of circuit training format (where you move straight from one exercise to other) during these sessions you perform 2-3 sets of one exercise before moving onto the next. Here are the parameters for this phase of the golf weight training program:

— Time of Year: Pre-season (to coincide with start of competitions)

— Phase Length: 6 weeks
— No. Sessions: 2 x week
— Session Length: 40-60min (inc. warm up/cool down)
— Resistance: 60% 1 repetition maximum
— Repetitions: 10-20
— Sets per exercise: 2-3
— Speed of lifts: Explosive

And the exercises:

1. Good Mornings to Shoulder Press x 10-12
2. Single Arm Dumbbell Rows x 12-15 (each arm)
3. Diagonal Medicine Ball Chop x 10-12 (each side)
4. Plyometric Push-Ups x 10-12
5. Dumbbell Squats and Rotational Swings x 10-12
6. Dumbbell Lateral Raises x 10-12
7. Standing Torso Twist x 10 (each side)
8. Reverse Crunch with Stability Ball x 20
9. Reverse Barbell Wrist Curls x 12-15
10. Barbell Wrist Curls x 12-15

Phase 3 - Maintain your newfound strength

During the off-season (ideally) you've built a solid base of strength, which will help to balance your musculature. You then progressed onto a more golf-specific, more demanding 6-week routine to help develop your power... Now the goal is to maintain those gains in strength and power that you've worked hard to develop.

The program below is an example of how you can achieve this. Of course it's always good to vary your program every 6 weeks or so. That you can avoid overworking certain muscle groups while neglecting others, plus it acts as mental stimulation.

Here are the parameters for this phase of the golf weight training program:

— Time of Year: In-season

— Phase Length: Indefinite

— No. Sessions: 1-2 x week

— session Length: 40-60min (inc. warm up/cool down)

— Resistance: 50-70% 1 repetition maximum (lighter loads for explosive exercises)

— Speed of lifts: Mixture of explosive exercises and controlled movements

And some sample exercises:

1. Alternating Squats with Press x 15
2. Lat Pull Downs (wide grip) x 15
3. Oblique Crunches x 20
4. Push-ups (or front press) x 15-20
5. Dumbbell Lunges x 10 (each leg)
6. Standing Torso Twist
7. Single Arm Dumbbell Rows
8. Diagonal Medicine Ball Chop
9. Back Extensions on Stability Ball x 20
10. Reverse Barbell Wrist Curls

Golf Strength Training

If you want hit the ball further, if you want play the game free of pain - following a golf strength training program should be high on your agenda.

— Every level of player wants to add 30-50 yards to their drives. Every golfer wants to start and finish each 18 holes without the all-too-common aches and twinges.

— Yet few - very few - golfers consider it important to condition themselves physically. And if they do consider it, it's a passing thought never to be acted on.

— Perhaps the old myth still persists - that all forms strength training results in bulky, tight muscles with limited range of movement. Not true. It takes a very specific type of weight training (plus diet) to bulk up - something we'll steer well clear of.

— Or maybe it's because physical make-up never relates to a person's handicap. Golf is played by such a wide range of people... from 8 years old to 80, overweight, thin, tall, short, fit and unfit... and they all compete on a level playing field.

— Yet with the right conditioning program everyone of those players would improve their game. If you're new to the game, following a golf strength training program will give you a solid and well-balanced base on which to build the fundamentals of a good swing.

— If you're a seasoned low-handicapper, strength conditioning can certainly give you a significant competitive edge and lower your handicap still further.

— If youth is still on your side - start a golf strength training program now and you can build a healthy, balanced body that stays free of chronic back pain, frozen shoulders and golfers elbow.

— And for the more senior players - it's never too late to redress the physical imbalances that have occurred through years of playing.

In this chapter we'll cover some of the basics of a good golf strength training program. Then at the end we'll move on to a sample golf weight training regimen that has helped many golfers improve their game.

Golf Strength Training Improves Shot Distance

From back swing to finish position a golf swing takes between 1 and 2 seconds. In that time a golfer's body generates some exceptional forces - potential energy that must be stored then released as efficiently as possible - and then you have to actually make contact with the ball!

The key to lengthening your shots is to increase the amount of force you can generate which in return, increases club head speed.

A study in 2004 of 45 golfers aged 18 to 80, showed that club head speed in recreational players correlated closely with handicap - the lower the handicap, the greater the club head speed found in a player's swing.

Two more recent studies measured whether an 8-week conditioning program could improve swing forces and club head speeds in golfers on all ages and abilities. The results showed that just 2 days per week of simple strength, power and flexibility exercises significantly increased club head speed and shot distance.

And these studies are by no means unique. What is clear is that physical conditioning will increase your distance with every club... more so than spending hours on the practise tee trying to swing faster and harder.

Golf Strength Training Reduces the Risk and Severity of Injury

As a rule of thumb most injuries that occur in golf tend to be over-use injuries of the soft tissues. Even fair-weather players repeat the same movement pattern thousands of times each year - on the course, at the driving range and of course the back yard.

And any similar explosive movement repeated over and over will train and condition some muscles whilst others are neglected...

At the most obvious level, the golf swing is performed in the same direction every time. Unequal forces are placed on one side of the body compared to other. That's why pros spend time swinging in the opposite direction - it's not just to prepare for those tricky shots when the ball lies flush against a tree!

And there are more subtle changes in posture and muscular balance that can occur over time. Muscles in the lower back might become overly strong compared to the abdominals for example. Larger muscle groups might develop at the expense of smaller, stabilising muscles, which puts them under a disproportional amount of strain.

It only takes a few weak muscles to cause postural changes over time, that weaken them further and so on in a downward spiral, until the result is chronic pain and over-use injury.

While a golf strength training routine is by no means a cure-all, it is perhaps the best solution for tackling the underlying cause. And if you take some time off each year and focus on restoring an optimal balance, there's no reason why you can't play pain-free golf right into your later years.

Foundations of a Golf Strength Training Program

You don't have to follow a time-consuming, highly regimented routine to benefit from strength training. But there are some important guidelines that set a golf strength program aside from simply lifting weights at the gym.

Split your routine into phases

Because most golfers are new to strength training, it's important they follow a period of functional training. This serves 2 purposes - firstly it prepares muscles, ligaments, tendons and connective tissue for more demanding exercise and secondly, it helps to target neglected, stabilising muscles.

This initial phase of a golf strength training program emphasizes core stability exercises and uses light weights and high repetitions. The ideal time to perform this 6-8 week phase would be during the off-season - those months were there are no club competitions and you can have a break from the game.

The next logical phase is to develop peak strength and power so that it coincides with the start of the competitive season. The intensity of exercises increases and more golf-specific movements are incorporated. In this phase we also have to...

Make strength training golf specific

The end goal of a golf strength training program is to develop golf-specific power. Increased strength does not necessarily translate into more power and faster club head speed. As a side note, don't confuse club head speed with swing speed. Trying to swing faster is not necessarily the answer to increasing length. Ernie Els has a classically slow-looking swing. He still generates enormous club head speed and distance. There are biomechanical reasons why swinging slower can actually increase club head speed at impact.

To take the idea of specificity a step further, does a bench press or biceps curl closely match the mechanics of the golf swing? No - what are more beneficial are exercises that include the whole body and incorporate the core region. And will exercises that cause rotation at the hips and core be more useful than those that don't. Absolutely!

Of course there is a caveat — in the early phase of the program, when a functional strength base is being developed, less golf-specific exercises are useful and help to counterbalance the repetitive nature of golf.

Incorporate specialist exercises for hard to target muscle groups

According several studies the most commonly occurring injuries in amateur golfers after back pain is golfer's or tennis elbow (caused by over-use and inflammation of the wrist flexors and extensors), wrist injuries and shoulder injuries (over-use and inflammation, or even partial tears of the rotator cuff muscles).

Perhaps the best way to prevent these injuries is to strengthen the forearm and rotator cuff muscles. By adding in a few choice exercises to specifically strengthen these areas, they become more resistant to over-use, tearing and inflammation. Of course if you already have an injury or pain you should consult your physician who will advise you on the best course of treatment.

Don't neglect elexibility

While the subject of stretching for golf is covered in another part it deserves mention here. A muscle can only contract as forcefully as its opposing muscle can relax. Stretching promotes relaxation in the muscles. Of course there are other important reason to stretch relating to injury prevention and improved swing mechanics.

Golf Stretching Program

By following a golf stretching program you will not only increase your power and reduce the risk of injury, it will also help you to maintain a more consistent swing pattern. And ultimately that means a lower handicap!

The golf stretching program set out below is designed to be completed either on days you aren't playing or after a round. It is not a suitable program to use as a warm up and there is a good reason for that.

This stretching program consists of static stretching exercises. While this is the best type of stretching for increasing range of motion it can compromise power immediately afterwards. Just as lifting heavy weights just before a game would leave your muscles temporarily tired and weak, static stretching immediately prior to teeing off can also negatively effect your shot distance and swing mechanics.

Guidelines

— You should be completely warm before starting this routine. Do 5-10 minutes of brisk walking or jogging on the spot to increase heart rate and pump blood to the major muscle groups.

— Perform the stretches in the order below.

— Hold each stretch for 20 seconds, relax and then repeat for another 20 seconds before moving on to the next stretch.

— The muscle group being stretched should feel slightly tight diminishing as you hold the stretch.

— Cease the stretch immediately if you feel any pain or if tightness increases as you stretch.

— Remember to breathe as this promotes relaxation and prevents an increase in blood pressure!

— Perform this routine a minimum of 3 days a week for 6 weeks - ideally 5-7 days is best.

Golf Stretching Program

Dynamic stretches

Start with some arm circles - perhaps 10 clockwise and 10

counter-clockwise. Next do some twisting from side to side - keep your feet shoulder width apart, place your hands on your hips or at chest height and turn from side to side 15-20 times. These dynamic stretches just help to increase blood flow and loosen joints before moving onto the static stretches.

Shoulder and chest stretch

This can be performed kneeling or standing. Clasp hands behind back and straighten arms. Raise hands as high as possible and bend forward from the waist and hold.

Shoulder stretch

Place one arm straight across chest. place hand on elbow and pull arm towards chest and hold. Repeat with other arm.

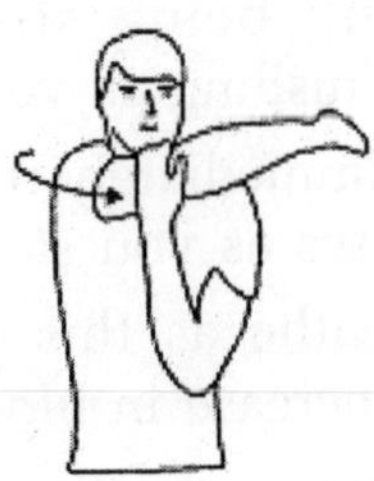

Triceps stretch

Place one hand behind back with elbow in air. Place other hand on elbow and gently pull towards head. Hold and repeat with other arm.

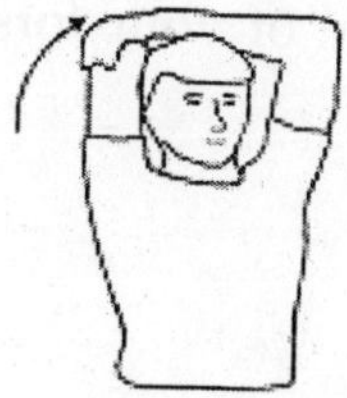

Chest stretch (Wall)

Place an outstretched arm against a wall or doorway and lean forward with that shoulder. You should feel a stretch in your chest when you lean forward. Hold and repeat for same arm then repeat 2 stretches for other arm.

Back stretch

1. Start by kneeling on the ground with your arms out in front of you.

2. Slide your arms further away and slowly shift your hips back towards your feet until a comfortable stretch is felt.
3. Now slide your hands to the right until a stretch is felt down the side of your torso. Repeat to the left.

Low back stretch

1. Lie on back with right knee drawn toward chest.
2. Slowly bring bent leg across body until a stretch is felt in the lower back and hip area.

3. Remember to keep shoulders squared and flat on ground at all times. Bottom leg should be bent so that your knees are aligned.

Butterfly stretch

1. Sit in upright position and place heels together.
2. Spread knees apart and pull feet toward groin until a stretch is felt in groin and inner thigh.

3. Remember to keep low back straight to emphasize stretch.

Hamstring stretch

1. Sit in upright position. Tuck foot near groin with opposite leg straight.
2. Bending from the hips and leading with the chest, reach down until a stretch is felt in back of thigh.
3. Remember to keep the low back straight to isolate stretch in hamstring

Quad stretch

1. Standing with a shoulder width stance and hang onto an object for support.

2. Bring one foot up and grab with your hand.
3. Pull your foot up until you feel a stretch on the front of your thigh.
4. Hold, relax and repeat before changing legs.

Forearm/wrist stretch

Stand with your right arm extended straight out. Pull back your fingers with the other hand until you feel a stretch in your forearm. Hold, repeat and then repeat 2 stretches on other arm.

These golf stretching exercise, performed regularly will help to promote relaxation in the muscles. This has the added benefit of also increasing body awareness, which is so important for maintain a consistent swing pattern.

Additionally, the more a muscle group can relax, the more forcefully its opposing muscles group can contract. Coupled with a suitable strength training program these golf stretching exercises will help to increase you power with every club.

Golf Stretching Exercises (Before a Round)

Golf stretching exercises, performed consistently (and properly) will increase your range of motion, your power and ultimately... help to reduce your handicap. Perhaps just as importantly, stretching will help to reduce the occurrence of those niggling injuries that so many golfers must endure. However there are different types of golf stretching exercises and which ones you perform, and when, makes a significant difference.

The stretching exercises on this page are designed just prior to a game - as part of a warm up routine. The majority are dynamic stretches which will help to reduce muscle stiffness without compromising your power.

There are several other forms of stretching - the most common being static stretching and this is great for increasing your flexibility. But more and more research is showing that static stretching before a sport that involves powerful movements (such as the golf swing) can negatively affect performance. Simply put, this type of stretching reduces how powerfully you can contract your muscles and so potentially, how far you can hit the ball.

For this reason athletes in most sports are now advised to warm with dynamic stretches and increase their flexibility either on separate days, or after a game, with static stretches. Complete this pre-game warm up and golf stretching exercises in the order set out. It should take no longer than 10-15 minutes and it's important you get to the course early to allow for this.

Golf Stretching Exercises and Warm Up Routine

Start this routine about 15-20 minutes before you tee-off. It loses its effect if you spend 15-20 minutes afterwards getting your bag and clubs together. You should be changed and ready to play so that you tee-off within 5 minutes of finishing this warm up.

Step 1 - Walking for 3-5 minutes

Walk briskly for 3-5 minutes, either around the car park or a quiet area of the course. You might want to walk from your car to the locker room and back a few times.

Step 2 - Supported squats

This exercise will elevate your heart rate and increase blood flow to the major muscle groups.

1. Hold a short club (i.e. 8 iron) overhead with hands at either end. Arms should be fully stretched directly above you.
2. Squat down until your thighs are almost parallel to the ground and stand up. Repeat 10 times.
3. Rest and repeat again.

Advanced players you can do this supported, single leg squat instead.

1. Start by standing and bracing against a golf club such as a 2 or 3 iron.

2. Bring your left foot up and place across your opposite knee. Your knee will be bent at 90 degrees.
3. Squat down until your knee is almost parallel to the ground, stand up and repeat 10 times.
4. Return to the starting position and repeat with the other leg.

Step 3 - Golf stretching exercises

Complete the following stretches in order.

Arm swings

1. Stand tall and hold arms out to your side.
2. Slowly swing your arms back and forth across the front of your body.
3. Repeat this continuous motion for 30 seconds.

Trunk rotations

1. Stand with a shoulder width stance. Place a club on your shoulders holding it at either end.
2. With knees slightly bent, bend forward from the waist slightly (as though adopting the swing posture).
3. Turn from side to side aiming to get the ends of the club directly in front of you with each turn.
4. Complete a total of 15-20 full swings.

Side bends with club

1. Stand with a shoulder width stance. Place a club on your shoulders.

2. Lean to one side keeping your torso straight. Do not bend forward or backwards.
3. Hold for a count of 2 and then repeat to the other side.
4. Complete 8-10 stretches each side.

Standing shoulder stretch

1. Stand with a shoulder width stance and place both hands on the end of the club.
2. Lean forward keeping your back flat until you feel a stretch in your shoulders.
3. Hold for 10 seconds and relax. Repeat a total of 3 times.

Leg swings

1. Start by standing with your feet shoulder width apart.
2. Keeping your upper body perpendicular to the ground swing one leg forward and backward.
3. Do not swing your leg so hard that you can not keep your upper body from moving. 4. Repeat for 10 full swings and repeat on other leg.

Alternate Toe Touches

1. Start by standing with your feet spread as far apart as comfortably possible.
2. Lean forward toward one leg and try to reach your foot or until a comfortable stretch is felt in your low back and hamstrings.
3. Now try to touch the other foot with the opposite arm. Ths motion should be continuous alternately touching each foot with the opposite hand.

Wrist extensions

1. Stand with your right arm extended straight out.
2. Pull back your fingers with the other hand until you feel a stretch in your forearm.
3. Hold for 10 seconds and repeat with the other wrist. Repeat again for each wrist.

Weighted club

Using either a weighted club or 2 clubs held together perform 10 complete swings. However, rather than stopping between each swing, it should be one continuous motion. For example, start with a back swing into a full follow through and immediately from the finish position take the club into the back swing position.

Step 4 - Practice swings

Complete 2-3 minutes of practice swings working on any techniques, or swing thoughts you may have been given. It's important not to practice technique with a weighted club or two clubs at this stage. You are now warmed up physically and this time is about sharpening your swing and reminding yourself of any coaching points to work on during the round. It is also a good idea to rest completely for about 2 minutes before you tee-off. Avoid walking up to the tee out of breath as this will compromise your ability to control your swing.

11

Soccer Training

Soccer is perhaps the most demanding of all sports. In the modern game (at any level) soccer training and conditioning is essential. Few sports are played on as large a playing field, lasting as long and without regular rest periods. Players cover 8-12km during a match, consisting of 24% walking, 36% jogging, 20% coursing, 11% sprinting, 7% moving backwards and 2% moving whilst in possession of the ball.

Soccer players posses excellent endurance with VO2max reported to range between 55 and 70 ml/kg/min in elite performers. The game is played at an average intensity close to the lactate threshold - approximately 80-90% of maximum heart rate.

How important is the correct type of endurance training in soccer? The greater a player's aerobic capacity, the more ground they cover during a typical game. Additionally, improved endurance also increases the number of sprints completed in a game. By improving the VO2max of youth soccer players by 11% over an 8 week period, a 20% increase in total distance covered during competitive match play was manifested, along with a 23% increase in involvements with the ball and a 100% increase in the number of sprints performed by each player.

What about other forms of conditioning? Strength training now plays a major role in soccer. However, simply lifting weights with the traditional "3 sets of 10 repetitions" approach is not an efficient way to spend training time. Soccer requires a balance of explosive power and muscular endurance. Some players may benefit from increasing their lean mass but even they should focus on converting much of their strength into soccer-specific power.

Strength training for soccer also helps to correct muscle imbalances. Soccer players in particualr are prone to developing overly strong quadriceps in relation to their hamstrings and a well-formed strength plan can address this and prevent future injury.

12 Month Soccer Training Program

Step 1 — ask yourself honestly how much time you are willing to commit to your soccer training program. Then take a bit off to account for over enthusiasm!

Step 2 — what is your current level of conditioning? Be more precise than "fit" or "unfit". Which elements of fitness do you need to work on most? Speed? Strength? Endurance? If you don't know...

You can do these in one afternoon and it's well worth the effort. Of all the different types of soccer training you could perform (strength training, speed training, skill work etc.) 20% will make 80% of the difference to your game. Stay on the right side of the 80/20 principle. Build your soccer training program around those areas that need most improvement, especially if your time is limited.

Even if you only play 8 months of the year, your soccer training program should stretch the entire 12 months. More on why in a moment. The first thing to do is split up our program into 4 distinct phases.

— Early pre-season soccer training
— Late pre-season soccer training
— In-season soccer training
— Closed or off-season soccer training

If you simply want to improve your fitness over the summer - ready for trials next season - base your program on the late pre-season phase. Side Note At this stage don't worry about individual sessions. This is the "big picture" - how all the different types of training fit together.

Professional players might not see a ball for the first half of the pre-season. The emphasis is on preparing yourself for the more demanding, late pre-season soccer training. At this early stage break keep things light and not too demanding. The last thing you should do is dive straight into all out, stomach wrenching interval training!

Endurance Training

Stick to predominantly continuous type training. This is lower intensity aerobic conditioning. Continuous training should be the only form of endurance training you perform for the first 2-3 weeks. Gradually progress to more intense interval training as you move into late pre-season.

Strength training

Ideally you want to develop maximum strength a few weeks before the start of the competitive season. Why? Before you can develop explosive power and even speed you must first develop a solid strength base. Maximum strength can take up to 12 weeks to develop so if strength is a priority for you, start your strength training during the off-season.

Speed and power training

No need for any speed or power work at this stage. Leave it until the late pre-season and In-season.

Flexibility

Don't under estimate the importance of flexibility in a soccer training program. Unfortunately most soccer players do. Flexibility training is essential for recovery and injury prevention. The best players in the World are useless on the sidelines!

Again you'll find some good soccer stretching exercises you can use to increase your range of movement below. And do remember there stretching to improve flexibility is not the same as stretching during a warm up. There are some key differences.

Skill And tactical training

The amount of skill work you do at this stage depends on the amount of time you have available. Players old enough to perform demanding fitness training (Over 16) will have a relatively high level of skill.

Late Pre-Season (4-6 weeks)

A word of warning - these few weeks might have you asking, "Why didn't I take up golf?" but this is the phase of your soccer training program that will have the greatest impact on your game... from a fitness perspective.

Endurance training

By now, all of your endurance training should be in the form of interval training. Your soccer training should also become more specific during the late pre-season. Try to match the movement patterns you would find in a typical match. For example: Keep the intervals short and intense, include twists and turns and running backwards, train on grass and juggle a ball during active recovery periods etc.

Strength training

Gradually decrease the number of strength sessions and replace them with power training sessions such as plyometrics. Plyometric training can be extremely effective at developing power and explosive off-the-mark speed but is not suitable for everyone. Again, don't worry too much if "plyometric training" means nothing to you. We're still on the "big 12-month picture".

Speed training

As the competitive season draws closer your soccer training should place more and more emphasis on quickness and sharpness. Again your conditioning must be soccer specific. Vary your sprint starts for example, by running backwards for a few yards first, jumping to head a ball or controlling and passing a ball before sprinting etc.

Flexibility

As the volume and intensity of your soccer training increases flexibility training becomes even more essential.

Skill and tactical training

Combine skill work with some of your fitness training to save time. If you plan to do an intense interval training session do your skill work first. If you plan to combine plyometrics or sprint drills with skill work always perform the plyometrics or sprints first. It goes without saying.

The warm up should precede all of these. Before we move on to In-Season training phase take a look at the chart below. It will give a quick reference as to how all the different elements of soccer fitness integrate over a season.

Priority Of Fitness Elements in a Soccer Training Program

	Early Pre-Season	*Late Pre-Season*	*In-Season*
Continuous training	High	Low	Low
Interval training	Low	High	Maintenance
Strength training	High	Moderate	Low
Power training	High	Moderate	Maintenance
Speed training	Low	High	Maintenance
Flexibility training	High	High	High

Closed Season Training

Nearly there! Avoid abandoning all forms of physical conditioning now the season has ended. If you do nothing for 6 weeks much of the hard work you've put in over the last season will be lost.

Do what professional players are advised to do. Cross-training... or X-Training as it's also known. Do some other form of activity that keeps your fitness levels ticking over and gives you a mental break from soccer. Swimming, cycling, tennis, basketball - any of these are good alternatives. Try to exercise 3 times a week for at least 30 minutes. Let's quickly sum it all up in one small table that covers the 12-month calendar.

Phases In A 12 Month Soccer Training Program

Month	May	Jun	Jul	Aug	Sep	Oct	Nov	Dec	Jan	Feb	Mar	Apr
Phase	CS	CS	EPS	LPS	IS	IS	IS	IS	IS	IS	IS	IS

CS = Closed season soccer training, EPS = Early pre-season soccer training, LPS = Late pre-season soccer training, IS = In season soccer training.

Splitting the soccer training program up this way really is the most effective approach to conditioning. And it will give you a tremendous advantage over other players and teams.

Soccer Strength Training

Few players get soccer strength training right. Today's soccer performers must be "complete athletes". They have to be quick off the mark and over 10-20 yards. They have to have the upper body strength to resist challenges. They need excellent levels of both aerobic and anaerobic endurance to last the duration.

If you simply lift weights - in much the same way as a bodybuilder - you are doing yourself and your game a great disservice. Bodybuilders, and athletes whose sports are predominantly strength based, will train to increase size, bulk and maximal strength. They're not too concerned if it's to the detriment of their aerobic endurance levels or even their agility and flexibility.. If all you do is follow the typical 3 sets of 8-12 repetitions all year round, you are far from getting the most from your soccer strength training sessions.

Different Types of Soccer Strength Training

In soccer, lower body strength is required for kicking, jumping, tackling, twisting and turning and also forms the foundation for explosive speed.

Upper body strength is required for shielding the ball, holding off opponents, throw-ins and also contributes to overall power and explosiveness. We can split "strength" into three broader categories.

Absolute or maximal strength

Absolute strength is the maximum force that a muscle group can exert in single, momentary contraction. For example, a player who can leg press 250lbs has greater absolute strength than a player who can leg press 200lbs.

In soccer, good maximal strength is beneficial for holding off opponents and shielding the ball. More importantly it also forms the foundation of muscular speed and power. But there's a caveat. Maximal strength (usually measured by one repetition max) makes no allowances for time - for example, a weightlifter can spend 30 seconds or more slowly lifting a weight inch by inch. Not much use to the soccer player. As a rule of thumb then, maximal strength training serves a greater purpose than just increasing absolute strength. The end result should be to increase your explosive speed and power.

Muscular power

Power is a product of both absolute strength and the speed of movement. Increase either one (without lowering the other) and you increase explosive power. Yes, if you do nothing but follow a generalised weights routine you find in nearly every issue of popular fitness magazines, you will increase your power. That, of course, assumes you continue to maintain your speed and flexibility. But even those generalised programs can be enhanced if you consciously increase the speed of contraction.

Another, highly effective form of power training is called plyometrics. Plyometrics bridges the gap between strength and speed by combining elements of both in single movement patterns. It sounds complicated but it's not. In fact it's a very easy form of training to perform so long as the player and coach rigidly adhere to the guidelines.

As we'll see in a moment, soccer strength training should fall into some distinct phases. The first phase is used to develop a solid functional strength base in the off-season. You can then move on to a maximal strength phase before converting this into soccer-specific power or.

Strength endurance

Strength or muscular endurance is the ability of a muscle group to perform repeated, high-intensity movements. Strength endurance is essential for soccer - and like power, perhaps more essential than all-out strength. At some point in your soccer training routine you should focus on developing strength endurance. Going back to our 3 sets of 8-12 reps example, general weights programs are inefficient at best for developing soccer-specific strength endurance.

A much more efficient set-up is circuit training. And if you can incorporate stations into the circuit that match the movement patterns in soccer, you are way ahead of the game! With all these different types of soccer strength training, things can start to get a bit overwhelming. How do you train for maximal strength and power and muscular endurance - especially when you have limited training time? Obviously, the answer is you don't. Not even professional players can... or should. Instead, we break a soccer strength training program into several phases - each lasting between 4 and 12 weeks.

4 Phases of a Soccer Strength Training Program

It's crucial that you take a long-term perspective in your soccer strength training plan. Even if you only do 1 weights session a week, you should still adapt it over the course of your season. Looking at the big picture, so to speak, will help you see how it all fits together. It also takes the pressure off trying to cater for everything in just a few training sessions - a sure-fire way path to over training and not much of anything else. Here's an example of how you can break a season, and a soccer strength training program, into just a few manageable phases.

The off-season - build functional strength

Soccer, like any sport, places a lot of uneven demands on the body. Most players have a predominant kicking foot for example. They kick using the same motor patterns, tens of thousands of times every year. And so, some muscles develop more than others. Some joints are placed under more stress than others. The goals of this phase are:

— To prepare the joints, muscles, ligaments and tendons for more intense work in subsequent phases
— To strengthen underused stabiliser muscles
— To balance the right and left side of the body
— To redress the balance between the flexors and extensors (soccer players, for example, are notorious for having over-developed quads from repetitive kicking actions. No wonder hamstring injuries are so prevalent in the game).

A good portion of your soccer strength training should focus on core stability. It's a form of training that is becoming more and more popular, and rightly so. The core - the abdominals, lower back and trunk - all form your "center of power". Every twisting, turning , stopping and starting movement is supported by your core. It allows your upper and lower body to work in cohesion, minimising shock and stress.

This is the most important phase of any soccer strength training program. Yet most athletes dismiss it. And it becomes doubly important for younger players. The foundations you lay in this phase literally determine the quality of strength and power formed in later phases. More importantly, without this phase, injures - both short and long-term become much more likely.

Off-season/early pre-season - build maximal strength

With a good foundation to build on, you're fully prepared to move into phase 2... building maximal strength. This is where most players finish - the same routine (or some slight variation) all year round.

The goal of this phase is to develop the highest force possible. Since power is our overall outcome, it makes sense to develop strength first and then convert it into soccer-specific power.

The aim is to complete this phase before the start of the season. That way the latter stages of pre-season training can focus on power and strength endurance training.

More On Strength and Conditioning For Soccer

All the phases and types of soccer strength training are laid out step-by-step in Total Soccer Fitness, Sports Fitness Advisor it contains dozens of sample strength, power and muscular endurance programs to cater for a wide variety of needs - sets, repetitions, progression, exercise illustrations and so on. Not only that it outlines in detail all the elements of fitness crucial for succer on the soccer pitch. Including:

— Strength and strength endurance training
— Speed and agility training
— Aerobic and anaerobic endurance training
— Flexibility, warming up and cooling down
— Testing soccer-specific fitness
— Nutrition for soccer
— Off-season, pre-season and in-season program design

Sample Soccer Weight Training Program

Take just a little time to plan your soccer weight training program correctly and it will certainly re-pay ten-fold on the field. We also covered why a soccer weight training program consists of several phases over the course of a season. It doesn't matter what you play to - if you train with weights there's no reason why should adjust your routine as the year progresses.

Sample Soccer Weight Training Routine

One of the most efficient and effective set ups for strength endurance is circuit training.

By its very nature it builds both strength and endurance. Most of us are familiar with some form of circuit training but for the uninitiated here's a recap of the general guidelines:

— Lower weights and higher repetitions - the resistance should be about 50% of one repetition maxiumu (1-RM) or light enough to perform 15-25 repetitions. Very often body weight is enough resistance.

— Time is often used instead of repetitions - rather than prescribing a set number of reps, each exercise can be performed for a set period of time (i.e. 30 seconds).

— Short rest periods between exercises - to develop endurance, minimal rest is allowed between each stations and circuits.

— Alternate bodyparts - each station should work a different part of the body from the station before - ideally upperbody, lowerbody, upperbody and so on.

The routine:

Reps: 30sec per station

Circuits: 2-3

Rest between stations: 20-30sec

Rest between circuits: 2min

Increase the intensity gradually over a period of weeks by increasing the time per exercise/station (45-60sec) or decreasing the rest periods. For exercises that use freeweights gradually increase the weight as it becomes easier.

Alternative Starts

The basis of these soccer speed drills is a 10-20 yard sprint. You start focus on accelerating as quickly as possible by powering away with your arms and legs. If this is a team session, make it more interesting by have 2 or 3 players sprint against each other.Alternate the start to make it more soccer-specific. Here are some ideas...

— Do 1-3 push ups, squat thrusts or burpees and sprint
— Start by kneeling, lying face down, sitting on your hands (which you're not allowed to use to get up) and sprint
— Do 5 keep ups or 5 ball touches and sprint
— Have some one throw or pass your the ball for you to control and lay off and sprint
— Run backwards for 5yards and turn and sprint
— Touch left hand down, touch right hand down, jump to head the ball and sprint

Speed Ladder

Speed ladders are simple pieces of equipment that allow athletes to develop fast feet and co-ordination. Drills include:

— High-knee running with very short strides

— Side steps in and out of the side of the ladder
— Bounding from one section to another

Stepping Strides

1. Place a series of markers on the ground about 1 yard apart for a total of 10 yards.
2. From a standing start run the length of the markers as fast as possible but making sure to take one stride (one ground contact) between each marker.
3. Move the markers closer together and repeat. Now move them further apart and repeat. Each time focus on taking only one stride between each marker.

Over Speed Training

Rather than working on power, these soccer speed drills develop leg speed movement and co-ordination. A simple drill to promote over speed is to run down hill. It should be a very slight hill, anything more and form is lost and the injuries are gained!

A small, grassy embankment is ideal. Again keep sprints to 10 yards. You buy something called a speed harness - rubber bungees that pull you along. But you really don't need for soccer.

Resistance Speed Training

This is the opposite to over-speed drills. Here the emphasis is on developing leg power over the first few yards. An incline (again grassy embankments are good) of about 30 degrees is ideal. You may need longer recovery between reps as these drills are more intense.

Resistance parachutes have the same effect but they are expensive and not practical for group training. Some pro soccer teams train on sand dunes - uphill and down hill. This is ok for pre-season work and will build muscular endurance. But they are not suitable for speed sessions as you can imagine.

Endurance Soccer Training Guideline

There are a few key principles (called the principles of training) that are particularly relevant to aerobic endurance conditioning...

Specific

The mode of training you perform should be specific to your sport. So, as an obvious example, soccer players run. Cycling or swimming will develop aerobic endurance but not in the same precise manner that jogging will.

Overload

An endurance soccer training session must be strenuous enough to overload the aerobic system. By overload I simply enough intensity to take your body out of its comfort zone. The caveat is that you don't try and follow a "no pain - no gain" mentality!

Progression

As your body adapts to vigorous training it will soon fall into a comfort zone again. To continue improving you must progress the intensity (or duration) to bring about more overload and so more adaptation.

Recovery

Over-training is not a past time reserved only for the elite. It is easy to do too much and try to progress too quickly. Listen to your body. Be flexible with your plan and take a day off if needs be. Or lighten the intensity for a week to boost your energy levels.

In early pre-season, light endurance soccer training might feature 5 or 6 days of the week for pros. Three is ample.

As the season start draws closer, a program might consist of 3 higher intensity interval sessions per week. Each endurance session should last between 20 and 45 minutes. After 45 minutes returns are diminished and it begins to impact on other training modalities.

Continuous and Interval Endurance Soccer Training

Aerobic endurance sessions can be split into 2 broad groups:

— Continuous training - running at a moderate intensity continuously, without rest periods

— Interval training - higher intensity for shorter bouts separated by rest periods

Which of these 2 types of aerobic endurance training is more specific to soccer? Yep... interval training. Soccer is played in short bursts.

That doesn't make continuous training obsolete though. It is the best from of conditioning for early pre-season when players return form the off-season break. It is also used for active recovery sessions - maybe the day after a particularly tough game. Fartlek training offers a nice variation and is great for group training.

It consists of running, jogging and walking intermittently. For example a player could cruise for 30 seconds followed by a light jog for 60 seconds, followed by a three quarter sprint for 10 seconds.

This cycle is repeated for the duration of the session - 20 to 30 minutes on averageThere is any number of combinations for fartlek training. It's a good introduction to the training season and adds variety to the often monotonous, continuous endurance training.

Interval training becomes more important in the latter stages of pre-season preparation. Interval endurance sessions, being more intense, tend to be shorter in time than continuous runs. During the in-season a competitive game acts as an interval endurance session. Usually that is enough to maintain the aerobic conditioning built up during pre-season preparation. One extra session per week is fine also.

Anaerobic Endurance Soccer Training

Moving away from aerobic endurance there is another type of endurance very important to you, as a soccer player:

— It's called anaerobic endurance. Your ability to maintain short bursts of power or repeat high-intensity movements in quick succession is a measure of your anaerobic endurance.

— If you take time to train for improved speed endurance it can have a dramatic effect on your game. It's tough. In fact it's by far the toughest form of training I have had the good fortune to complete!

— If you've never enjoyed the effects of sudden and significant amounts of lactic acid running through your blood stream, you are in for a treat!

— But in comparison it makes a competitive game feel easy. It does wonders for your confidence. And your touch and skill improves as a bonus.

— There is nothing more difficult than trying to control a difficult ball and make an accurate pass when you are gasping for breath. With this type of training you rarely struggling making the rest of the game that much more enjoyable.

Off Season Soccer Training

Off season soccer training has two important objectives:

1. Physical recuperation and mental respite from a strenuous season

2. Minimise any losses in strength and conditioning built up over the year.

In fact one of the World's leading strength experts Tudor Bompa, suggests that "off season" is an inappropriate name. Instead he calls it the "transition phase" between two 12month programs.

The worst thing you can do during this time is nothing - especially if you have worked hard to build up your strength and fitness levels over the season. Remember, maintaining 50-60% of your peak fitness level takes less effort than starting from scratch.

And if you do nothing for just 5-6 weeks you will be starting from scratch.

Just as detrimental as doing nothing is maintaining your routine through the closed season. You must give your body (and mind) a rest. Even if you feel fresh enough to continue through the off season months, do so and mid way into the following season you could feel completely burnt out.

An off season soccer training program should also focus on rebalancing the body. Chances are you have a predominant kicking foot. You've placed some muscles, tendons and joints under the same stresses time and time again. Now it's time to focus on stabilising neglected muscle groups.

The off season soccer training phase should last between 4 and 6 weeks. Less is not enough time for adequate rest. More and you begin to lose significant amounts of the soccer-specific fitness gained from the previous year.

The focus should be on light aerobic endurance exercise and, in some circumstances, some resistance training.

about 40mL.kg.min in males and 30mL.kg.min in females for the average population.How do soccer players fair? Have a look at the table below:

Average $VO2_{max}$ for Pro and Semi-Pro Soccer Players (mL.kg.min)

Position	*Full-back*	*Centre-back*	*Midfield player*	*Striker*	*Goalkeeper*
Professional players	62	56	62	60	51
Semi-professional players	55	55	58	54	n/a

Compared to the average population then, soccer players unsurprisingly have excellent endurance capacity. You can estimate your own $VO2_{max}$ with a simple soccer fitness test like a 12-minute run.

Speed and Agility in Soccer

Another significant component of a soccer fitness program is speed and agility training. The speed of play in today's game is said to be quicker than ever. While elite soccer players are by no means Olympic sprinters, all other things being equal, faster players have a marked competitive edge.

A very simple speed test is a sprint over 30 yards from a standing start. You can do this easily if you have someone time you. Take the average time over 3-4 sprints (with plenty of rest between attempts). Anytime under 5.0 seconds is good. Professional players average 4.0 seconds. Perhaps more important than all-out speed is speed endurance.

Flexibility in Soccer

Last and certainly not least is flexibility. In most cases

increasing your range of motion can be very beneficial - not only in the prevention if injury but to increase your speed, agility and power too.

Flexibility sessions should feature heavily in your soccer fitness regime. Measuring flexibility is a simple procedure. A test like the modified sit and reach, groin flexibility test or truck rotation test are all specific to soccer. You can also buy a large protractor called a goniometer to quickly measure the range of movement about a joint.

Soccer Fitness Training Tips and Sessions

Sport Fitness Advisor has recently developed Total Soccer Fitness - a comprehensive step-by-step guide to peak soccer performance. It covers all the important elements of fitness in depth:

— Strength and strength endurance training

— Speed and agility training

— Aerobic and anaerobic endurance training

— Flexibility, warming up and cooling down

— Testing soccer-specific fitness

— Nutrition for soccer

— Off-season, pre-season and in-season program design

Bibliography

Andersen, Mark B, *Doing Sport Psychology,* Human Kinetics, 2000.

Brockopp, Gene W. "Review of Research on Multi-Modal Sensory Stimulation with Clinical Considerations and Research Proposals. 1984.

Burke, Ed; Burke, Edmund R., *Cycling Health and Physiology : Using Sports Science to Improve Your Riding and Racing,* Vitesse Pr., 1999.

Cohn, Patrick J., *Peak Performance Golf: How Good Golfers Become Great Ones,* Contemporary Books, 2000.

Cooper, Andrew, *Playing in the Zone : Exploring the Spiritual Dimensions of Sports,* Shambhala, 1992.

Counsilman, James, E., *The Science of Swimming,* Englewood Cliffs, NJ: Prentice Hall, Inc., 1994.

Davies, Philippa, *Total Confidence,* London, England: Piatkus Publishing, 1994.

Dawson, Roger, *The 13 Secrets of Power Performance,* New Jersey: Prentice Hall, Inc., 1994.

Enos, Brian, *Practical Shooting,* Clifton, CA: Zediker Publishing, 1990.

Enhanger, Kjell, *Quantum Golf: The Path to Golf Mastery,* Warner Books, 1992.

Gawain, Shakti, *Creative Visualization : Use the Power of Your Imagination to Create What You Want in Your Life,* New World Library, 1995.

Johnson, Rebecca and Bill Tulin, *Travel Fitness,* Champaign, IL: Human Kinetics Publishing, 1958.

Liggett, Donald, *Sport Hypnosis,* Human Kinetics, 2000.

Maglischo, Ernest, *Swimming Faster,* Human Kinetics, 2001.

Miller, Saul; Hill, Peggy Maass, *Sports Psychology for Cyclists,* Velo Press, 1999

Singer, Robert N., *Handbook of Sport Psychology,* John Wiley & Sons, 2001

Whitten, Phillip. Ph.D., *The Complete Book of Swimming,* New York, NY: Random House, 1994.

Index

Abdominal exercises 45, 49
Advanced abdominal exercises 47
Anaerobic endurance 270
Autogenic inhibition 185

Ballistic action 85
Basic strength training programs 5

Chest dumbell exercises 95
Circuit training 224
Classical plyometric exercises 86
Concentric muscle actions 180
Continuous training 269
Core Strength Training 19

Diagonal woodchops 27
Dleayed Onset Muscle Sorness (DOMS) 186
Dumbell exercises 93
Dynamic Stretching 175

Endurance Training 256
Exercise selection 4
Explosive strength training 84, 86

Force-Velocity Relationship 81
Foundational strength 221
Free weights routines 9
Full-Body Kettlebell Training Program 32

Golgi Tendon Organs (GTO) 185

Hypertrophy 1, 6

In-season program design 264
Isometric exercises 51, 53

Kettlebell exercises 29
Kettlebell routines 9

Leg Dumbell Exercises 103
Long-Term Static Stretching Programs 178

Muscular Endurance Training 87

Periodisation 3
Plank supermans 49
Plyometric training 227
Plyometrics 86
PNF stretching 180
Power endurance 88
Power training 81

Range of Motion (ROM) 183
Resistance Band Exercises 24

Sample Stability Ball Exercises 43
Season Baseball Weight training 230
Self Myofascial Release Exercises 195
Self Myofascial Release Techniques (SMRT) 193
Soccer Strength Training 260
Sport Specific Approach 3
Sport-specific strength training program 1
Stability ball exercises 40
Static active flexibility 174
Static active stretching 176
Static strength training 51
Step-By-Step Strength Training Programs 9
Strength endurance 3, 12
Strength Training Program 1

Trapezius Dumbbell Exercises 107
Well-balanced foundation 222